SURV|
WORLD WAR TWO TANKS IN
THE ARDENNES

CRAIG MOORE

MILITARY VEHICLES AND ARTILLERY SERIES, VOLUME 4

Front cover image: In Bastogne town centre, an M4A3 Sherman Tank called 'Barracuda' is on display. It was knocked out during the Battle of the Bulge, 30 December 1944.

Title page image: In the hills above La Roche-en-Ardenne, there is a British M10 17pdr SP Achilles IIC.

Contents page image: The Tiger II tank at La Gleize, Belgium, was abandoned after its gun barrel was broken in half by a shell. It has been repaired.

Back cover image: An M4 Sherman Firefly tank turret sits on top of a tree trunk at the entrance of the private drive that leads to the Château d'Isle-la-Hesse, the 1944 Battle of the Bulge headquarters of the US Army 101st Airborne Division.

Acknowledgements

Adrian Barrel, Tim Bell, Mathieu Billa. Johnny Bona, Kevin Browne, Gerd Bruffaerts, Pierre-Oliver Buan, Lauren Child, Joshua Collins, Hilary Louis Doyle, Etienne Ducarme, Adam Gallon, Fabrice Gérardy, Max Hastings, Nigel Hay, Marcus Hock, Reg Jans, Bob Konings, Pascale Mathieu, Stephen MacHaye, Harry F Miller, Sue Moore, John Osselaer, Adam Pawley, Francis Pierard, Mark Ridgway, Jean Pierre Roels, William Testaert, Erwing Verholen, Anthony Wright, Krings Collection, Bastogne Barracks, Bastogne War Museum, Grandmenil.com, Norfolk Tank Museum, Panzer Farm, War Heritage Institute.

Published by Key Books
An imprint of Key Publishing Ltd
PO Box 100
Stamford
Lincs PE19 1XQ

www.keypublishing.com

Typeset by SJmagic DESIGN SERVICES, India.

Contents

Introduction

Travel tips

If you are going to make a long journey to see a specific tank highlighted in this book, make sure the tank is still there before you go. Tanks move. I know that sounds silly, but preserved surviving tanks used as memorials or museum exhibits are sometimes removed for restoration. On rare occasions, a few are temporarily transported to different locations to be displayed at World War Two anniversary events or used as part of a special exhibition. Send an e-mail to the local tourist board or Maire (Mayor). An internet search will provide you with the address. Check opening times before you visit museums. Some close for lunch, others are only open on certain days of the week and a few only open in the summer.

Not all of the tanks featured in this book are veterans from the December 1944 Ardennes Offensive, often called the Battle of the Bulge. Many tanks built during World War Two were used by the Dutch and Belgium armies during the early years of the Cold War. After they were replaced by more modern tanks, they were placed in storage, utilised as 'hard targets' on military firing ranges or presented to museums and towns to be used as historical exhibits or war memorials. When you see weapons damage on a preserved tank, it is very rarely the shell that put it out of action. Some were used as target practice after the crews had abandoned the vehicle. This happened to the Panther tank at Celles and the King Tiger at La Gleize. Turrets and tanks that have been recovered from a firing range display the scars of multiple post-war hits by rounds of various sizes.

US Army and Air Force units were involved in the majority of the fighting and suffered a larger percentage of Allied casualties. Some visitors are surprised to see British Sherman Firefly tanks and

A rare British-built World War Two Belgian Army Mk.II AEC armoured car.

self-propelled guns like the M10 17pdr SP Achilles IIC on display in the Ardennes. However, contrary to what Hollywood portrays, the British and Commonwealth, Free French and Belgian Army ground forces, along with RAF bombers and ground-attack aircraft, took part in the Battle of the Bulge. In December 1944, they defended the bridges over the River Meuse and then, in January 1945, went on the attack.

The Bastogne Barracks tank hall displays most of the Belgium War Heritage Institute (WHI) collection of World War Two armour. Unlike other museums in the area that concentrate on the Battle of the Bulge, the vehicles on display in Bastogne Barracks cover a period from 1939 to 1945. There are other types of vehicles on display, like the rare World War Two Belgian Army Mk.II AEC Armoured Car that was restored by William Testaert. Currently, there are also a few Cold War vehicles on display as well. If you are lucky, and it is open to visitors, you may be able to visit the Bastogne Barracks Vehicle Restoration Center workshop. Double-check visiting hours before you go by sending them an e-mail, as sometimes the website is not updated.

There are a large number of memorials to the fallen and the events of the Battle of the Bulge throughout the Ardennes. Old ones are being upgraded, and new ones are being commissioned; some feature artillery pieces. Recently, a World War Two US Army restored 8-inch howitzer was installed at the General Irzyk Park memorial in Chaumont, 11km south of Bastogne, between the farming villages of Grandru and Burnon. It came from the Belgium War Heritage Institute and was financed by the Chaumont community. There are also many military history museums and displays; some are large, and others are small – these are often found in the local council buildings or cafés. This guidebook concentrates on the surviving tanks in the Ardennes, where there is a lot to see and explore. The Ardennes is an attractive historic landscape that straddles the countries of Belgium and Luxembourg. You will need to spend at least two weeks in the area on your first visit.

This World War Two US Army 8-inch howitzer is part of the General Irzyk Park memorial in Chaumont, which is 11km south of Bastogne. (Erwin Verholen)

The Ardennes Offensive (16 December 1944 to 25 January 1945)

In the late summer of 1944, Hitler believed there was a great deal of dislike and distrust between the Allies. He felt that if he could drive a wedge between the Western Allies in a single penetrating attack, it would cause the fragile relationship to collapse. He hoped he could then avoid the demand for unconditional surrender, negotiate separate peace treaties with the Western Allies and so gain time to fight the Soviets in the east. The decision to launch the attack was his alone, and it was more political than military. After the failed von Stauffenberg bomb assassination attempt on 20 July 1940, Hitler needed to reassert his control over the German General Staff and all branches of the military. He knew the Allies' supply lines were stretched and were still operating from the beaches in Normandy. Although the critical large deep-water port of Antwerp was liberated on 4 September 1944, it could not be used to bring in supplies as the Germans still held the banks of the Scheldt River that flowed into the harbour. It took until 28 November 1944 for the port to start working again.

The plan was to attack westward through the heavily wooded undulating terrain of the Ardennes, cross the River Meuse and then head north to capture the port of Antwerp. The Allied 21st Army Group in the north would be encircled and destroyed, thus reducing the ground attack threat to the industrial Ruhr area of Germany. As part of a deception, in case plans fell into Allied hands, the operation was initially called *Unternehmen Wacht am Rhein* (Operation *Watch on the Rhine*), which suggested a defensive operation. Bogus units and call signs were used in communications. Military activity was increased in other areas of the front line to hide the build-up of forces near the Ardennes. Operational command was given to Field Marshal Otto Moritz Walter Model. He was allocated three armies: 6th Panzer Army was in the north, 5th Panzer Army in the middle and the 7th Army in the south. The spearhead of the attack was the 6th Panzer Army, whose instructions were to head straight for Antwerp after crossing the River Meuse. The 5th Panzer Army was to protect the flank of the spearhead by advancing via Brussels and stop the Allied reserves attacking the rear of the 6th SS Panzer Army. The 7th Army was given instructions to capture Luxemburg and protect the southern flanks of the operation.

It was important that the breakthrough to Antwerp was completed quickly because of the German's lack of fuel and supplies. Allied fuel dumps and the fuel reserves at the port of Antwerp needed to be captured for the plan to succeed. To be successful, the attack had to commence during a period of bad weather to negate the Allied air superiority.

Skorzeny's Commandos

Waffen-SS Commando Otto Skorzeny had commanded the successful raid to rescue deposed Italian leader Mussolini. He was put in charge of a specialised operation designed to ensure the early capture of the vital crossroads and bridges over the River Meuse in order to speed the advance of the 6th SS Panzer Army. Skorzeny's Commandos dressed in American army uniforms and drove captured Allied jeeps, a Sherman tank and five Panther tanks disguised as US 3-inch Gun Motor Carriage (GMC) M10 tank destroyers. Many, but not all, of the men were fluent in American English, some having lived in the US before the war. This deception was hoped to cause confusion, paranoia and distrust amongst the enemy, as they would not be able to tell who was friend or foe. It did have some success. Skorzeny and his men were well aware that, under the Hague Convention of 1907, if they were captured while wearing US uniforms, they could be executed as spies. Many were sentenced to death and shot by US Army firing squads. They did not capture any of the bridges over the River Meuse.

A post-war photograph of the Skorzeny's Commandos' disguised Panther Ausf. G, made to resemble American 3-inch GMC M10 tank destroyer number B5 of the 10th Tank Battalion, 5th Armored Division.

This is a German-operated Sherman tank used in the Ardennes in December 1944.

6th Panzer Army

The lead role in the attack was given to the 6th Panzer Army. It was assigned the shortest route to the primary objective, the critical Allied supply port of Antwerp. They had priority for equipment and supplies. In the attack plans, the Germans made a point of stating that troops would have to capture Allied fuel dumps to enable the Panzers to keep moving. Fuel was a major part of the German supply problem.

Freezing fog prevented the Allies from carrying out aerial reconnaissance. It was imperative to the success of the attack that the German troops moved quickly to capture their objectives before the enemy could mobilise reinforcements. Stubborn defence by US forces, narrow roads, missed fuel dumps, plus the failure to ignore and go around pockets of resistance slowed the advance. Kampfgruppe (Battle Group) Peiper was the spearhead of the 6th Panzer Army assault. They were delayed by 12 hours at the village of Lanzerath. To protect the panzers in the opening stage of the attack, the infantry was sent ahead of the tanks. They met resistance and started to dig in. When the tanks arrived, they found the American troops had left. The Germans pushed on to Honsfeld and made a detour north to capture the large fuel depot at Büllingen. At Baugnez, Kampfgruppe Peiper attacked and destroyed a column of 26 vehicles belonging to an artillery unit. In Malmedy, 84 out of 125 American prisoners, captured during the Battle of the Bulge, were killed when the Germans opened fire on them with machine guns. In and around Stavelot, the Germans massacred over 100 unarmed Belgian civilians after coming under fire from a US anti-tank unit that quickly left the village.

The Allies soon realised that the Germans were relying on capturing fuel during their advance to keep their vehicles moving, so they hurriedly set about destroying those in the path of the advance.

A new 90mm Gun Motor Carriage (GMC) M36 tank destroyer moving forward during heavy fog near Werbomont, Belgium, on 20 December 1944. They were usually issued to existing M10 Battalions, a company at a time, as they arrived from the factories.

Kampfgruppe Peiper began moving west out of Stavelot, completely missing a large intact fuel dump to the north of the village.

The 6th Panzer Army's reinforcement and supply lines were under threat of attack and artillery bombardment from the US troops occupying the Elesnborn Ridge on the north shoulder of the line of attack. The 12 SS-Panzer Division, supported by the 506th Heavy Panzer Battalion, was tasked with capturing the dominating piece of high ground. They could not dislodge the Americans.

US engineers blew up bridges in front of and behind the German spearhead, causing delays whilst new routes were found. The weather improved slightly, enabling Allied spotter planes to locate the advancing column and call in air and artillery attacks. With increasing resistance, the lack of fuel and the real risk of being cut off from reinforcements and supplies, the German attack gradually ground to a halt.

5th Panzer Army
Speed was essential for a successful outcome for the German attack. The determined, stubborn American defence of towns and villages like Hosingen, Consthum, Holzthum, Clervaux and Wiltz, which held out against vastly superior forces, seriously upset the German timetable. The plan had called for the capture and advance past Bastogne to secure bridge heads over the River Ourthe by the

In December 1944, the British XXX Corps were tasked with stopping the Germans from crossing the River Meuse. This Sherman Firefly tank is on the banks of the River Meuse in Namur.

end of the second day. Bastogne was an important transportation hub because of the web of roads that meet in the centre. The Germans called it a 'road octopus'. German forces only reached the outskirts of Bastogne on the fourth day of the attack. Hard fighting ensued with heavy casualties. With the defence perimeter around Bastogne holding, the German commanders were told to forget the city, move around it, and head for the bridges over the River Meuse. This additional delaying action had caused a fatal 48-hour interruption in the offensive's schedule. By the fourth day, the attack plan had expected the German advance to have reached and crossed the River Meuse. They had only covered a third of the expected distance.

On 20 December, the fifth day of the attack, more Allied units were being diverted to the area. The Supreme Commander of Allied Forces in Europe, General Dwight D Eisenhower, temporarily placed all units north of a line between the towns of Givet and Prum under the command of British Field Marshal Bernard Montgomery. He ordered the British XXX Corps, led by Lieutenant General Sir Brian Gwynne Horrocks, from Holland to join the Americans and stop the advancing Germans from crossing the River Meuse.

The spearhead of the German 5th Panzer Army, in the centre of the attack, was now gaining ground, having left the attack on Bastogne to other units. They were heading for Dinant on the banks of the River Meuse. On Christmas Eve, the village of Celles was captured by the Panzer Lehr Division, and to the north, the 2nd Panzer Division were in the village of Foy-Notre-Dame, only 4 miles (6.4km) away from the River Meuse. An Allied blocking force on the east side of the river prevented the Germans from advancing any further towards the vital bridges at Dinant, Givet and Namur over the River Meuse. This was the limit of the advance of the German 5th Panzer Army. They failed to cross the River Meuse.

This is Madame Marthe Monrique, standing in front of the Celles Panther at her restaurant called Le Tank. The sign is not historically correct. It says, 'Here, the von Rundstedt offensive was halted 24 December 1944.' This in fact occurred in the village of Foy-Notre-Dame.

The Allied Counter-attack

General Patton had already asked his staff to draw up plans for a northward turn to counter-attack the German offensive from the south, before being called to a meeting with General Eisenhower at his headquarters in Verdun on 19 December 1944. His Third Army was located in northeast France, south of the Ardennes. When asked how long it would take to start moving three divisions north, he shocked everyone by saying 48 hours, an unprecedently fast time. At 4.30pm on 26 December 1944, the lead element of Company D, 37th Tank Battalion, 4th Armored Division, part of Patton's Third Army, reached Bastogne, ending the siege. A general counter-attack by all Allied forces began on 3 January 1945.

By 8 January 1945, the German High Command, realising their attack had failed, and assailed by Allied counter-attacks, ordered their commanders to retreat toward Germany, but fighting continued against their rearguard. Eight days later, Field Marshal Montgomery ordered British XXX Corps back to the Netherlands.

Casualty estimates for the battle vary widely. The United States Department of Defense official estimate of American casualties is 89,500. The German High Command estimated they suffered between 81,834 and 98,024 casualties during the offensive. British and Canadian casualties were approximately 1,400.

It was the heroic stubborn resistance of small groups of American soldiers that caused serious delays to the German attack timetable that defeated the Germans. Their plan relied on speed and capturing Allied supplies. German troops wasted time clearing pockets of resistance rather than bypassing them and heading to the vital river crossings over the Meuse. The spearheads of both the 6th and 5th Panzer Armies ran out of fuel and had to abandon their tanks and vehicles.

This is an old postcard showing the M4A3 Sherman tank called Barracuda, on display in Bastogne Town Square.

An early post-war postcard of Clervaux Castle before its restoration and the M4A3(76)W Sherman tank on display outside, next to a captured German 88mm Pak 41/43 anti-tank gun.

A postcard showing the Houfflaize Panther Ausf. G Tank, photographed in the 1970s.

Map

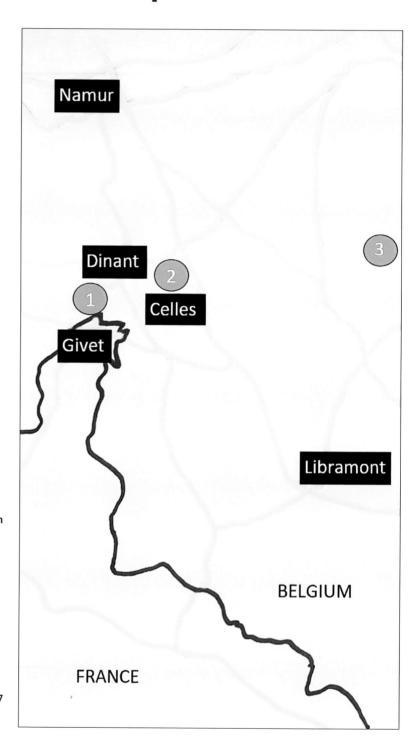

To help plan your exploration of the surviving World War Two tanks in the Ardennes, use these sketch maps. The green circles show the location of the tanks. The numbers indicate the chapter that provides information about the tank. The green ovals signify that there is more than one tank at this location. The chapter numbers are shown in a range: 6–8 at la-Roche-en-Ardenne, 14–37 at Bastogne and 40–44 at Diekirch.

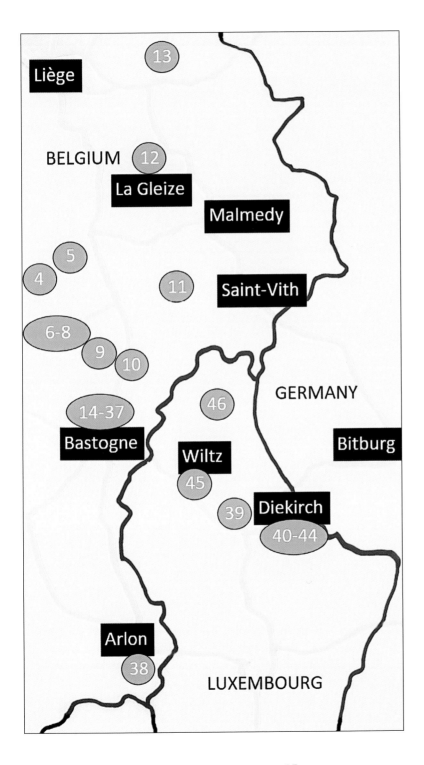

Chapter 1

Sherman VC Firefly Tank
Hermeton-sur-Meuse

Location: Set your navigation device to Rue de France 245, 5540 Hastière, Belgium. This is a garage 50m north of the tank. It is on the N96, 1.7km south of Hermeton-sur-Meuse.

The German Army planned to advance towards Antwerp in order to split the Allied forces. One of the most important parts of the plan was to take the bridges over the River Meuse. They failed, as British and American units defended the River Meuse. The Hermeton-sur-Meuse Sherman tank is positioned on the west bank of the River Meuse.

It is a British Sherman VC Firefly that was originally armed with the feared high-velocity Royal Ordnance Quick Firing (QF) 17pdr gun. This gun could knock out German heavy armour and was called a 17-pounder because that was the weight of the huge shells it fired. The Firefly was constructed using a converted M4A4 hull, serial number 4875, built by Chrysler in August 1942. The letter 'C' was added to the tank's 'Sherman V' designation to indicate that it was armed with a QF 17pdr gun. Notice there is no hull machine gun: additional space was required to stow the long 17pdr ammunition, so the hull machine gun was removed. It has the bracket for the gun clamp on the rear deck. This was necessary to lock the long barrel of the 17pdr gun into a fixed position during transportation, especially on a long drive outside a combat zone, to prevent it being damaged.

This tank replaced a M4A3E2(75) Sherman Jumbo tank, which had hitherto stood on this spot for over 50 years. The Jumbo has now been restored to a working condition (see Chapter 18). At the end of World War Two, the Sherman Jumbo was offered to dentist Dr Paul Michel, for use as a war memorial at Hermeton-sur-Meuse, in the commune de Hastiere, where Dr Michel had helped save lives by turning his house into a medical centre. The village of Hermeton-sur-Meuse agreed to the Jumbo's removal, but they still wanted a tank as a war memorial. The Royal Museum of Armed Forces and Military History in Brussels (now part of the Belgium War Heritage Institute) located the hull of a British Sherman Firefly that had seen service during the Cold War with the Belgian Army. Its 17pdr gun and turret had been destroyed beyond repair, so it was fitted with a standard 75mm gun turret. It was restored at the Belgian Army's Kapellen Depot. It is missing its gun mantlet.

Specifications	
Dimensions:	L: 25ft 9in (7.84m); W: 8ft 9in (2.66m); H: 9ft (2.74m); Wt: 32.1 tons (32.7 tonnes)
Engine:	Chrysler A57 30-cylinder, 4-cycle, multibank Petrol/gasoline 425hp engine
Crew:	4
Main armament:	QF 17pdr
Additional weapons:	.30cal Browning MG M1919A4 coaxial; .50cal Browning MG HB M2 flexible AA turret mount; 2in smoke bomb thrower
Armour thickness:	.75in to 3.5in (19mm to 89mm)
Max. road speed:	25mph (40km/h)
Total built:	Between 2,100 and 2,200

Chapter 2
Panther Ausf. G Tank
Celles

Location: Set your navigation device to the restaurant 'Le Tank', Route d'Achêne 1, 5561 Celles, Belgium. It is at the junction of the N94 with Route d'Achêne.

The Celles Panther was part of the German Army Kampfgruppe von Cochenhausen, 2nd Panzer Division. On 21 December 1944, the Panzer Lehr battle group was pulled out of the fight for Bastogne and regrouped with the 2nd Panzer Division and the 116th Panzer Division 'Windhund' for an assault on the important town of Dinant in order to secure the crossing over the River Meuse. On 24 December 1944, the advanced column of Panther tanks approached the road junction at Celles. The local story is that the Germans asked at the Pavillon des Ardennes café whether, if the road to Dinant was open, had vehicles been using it recently? The café owner, Madame Marthe Monrique, lied and said that it was mined and dangerous, so the Panther commander decided to go through the fields. This Panther Ausf. G was the lead tank. It drove over a mine and was put out of action in the field below the Chateau Acteau. The Germans temporarily stopped their advance. After the war, Madam Monrique became known as 'the woman who stopped the tanks'. A sign proclaims that the advance was stopped in Celles. This is not historically accurate.

In reality, the lead tank was knocked out by a mine; it was not the commander's Panther. This caused the Germans to stop and seek information from Madam Monrique. They carried on to Foy-Notre-Dame but discovered the British 3rd Royal Tank Regiment had blocked the roads to the bridge at Dinant near Sorinnes. The rest of the Kampfgruppe moved north to this location. RAF rocket-firing Typhoons attacked them. The US 2nd Armored Division attacked them from the east. Fighting was deadliest in Foy-Notre-Dame, around the Mayenne farm and in the orchards of Conneux-Conjoux. On 25 December 1944, low on fuel, they abandoned their vehicles only three miles from the river Meuse bridge at Dinant.

The disabled Panther at Celles was left in the field for some time after the war. At one point, it was turned upside down and stripped of its road wheels and tracks before being turned back onto its hull bottom again. The café owner recovered the tank from the field in 1948 and put it as a monument in pride of place at the crossroads, next to the cafe now renamed as 'Le Tank'.

Passing US forces tested anti-tank weapons on the abandoned tank. One shell hit the bottom of the curved gun mantlet, and it ricocheted down into the hull machine gunner's position through the hull deck. They were verifying the rumours that this area was a shell trap and a Panther tank's weak spot.

Specifications	
Dimensions:	L: 29ft (8.80m); W: 11ft 2in (3.42m); H: 10ft 2in (3.10m); Wt: 44.78 tons (45.5 tonnes)
Engine:	Maybach HL 230 P30 V12, water-cooled, 600hp petrol/gasoline engine
Crew:	5
Main armament:	7.5cm Kw.K.42 L/70, 82 rounds
Additional weapons:	Two 7.92mm M.G.34 machine guns
Armour thickness:	0.6in to 3in (16mm to 80mm); (Turret front and mantlet 4in to 4.3in/100mm to 110mm)
Max. road speed:	28.5mph (46km/h)
Total built:	2961 approx.

Chapter 3
Sherman VC Firefly 17pdr Tank Turret
Hotton

Location: Set your navigation device to Rue Haute 43, 6990 Hotton, Belgium. The turret is opposite this house near La Command'Rie restaurant.

O n 20 December 1944, there was a lot of fighting around the town of Hotton between US troops and the advancing Germans. An account by First Sergeant Maynard Dilthy, Company B (or 'Baker'), 23rd Armored Engineer Battalion, recalls that an advancing German column approaching the river bridge along a narrow riverside road was blocked when the leading tank was knocked out by a 57mm anti-tank gun. The Germans were forced to back up and look for alternative routes. Whilst they did that, the American infantry and engineers were joined by a 3-inch GMC M10 tank destroyer. It knocked out another German tank that was now approaching the bridge between two houses. The M10 then managed to knock out three more tanks. Fighting continued until Christmas day, when the Germans withdrew from the bridge area.

Units of the 53rd (Welsh) Infantry Division and supporting tanks managed to stop the Germans before they could cross the bridges over the River Maas, near Hotton. To commemorate these events, a monument in the shape of a turret from a Sherman Firefly can be found next to the N807 (Hotton/ Erezée) road. This road also marks the boundary of how far the German advance had reached during the Battle of the Bulge (one exception was the long narrow advance from Marche-en-Famenne to Celles). The plaque on the memorial reads: 'In tribute to the gallant soldiers of the 53rd Welsh Infantry Division and their attached armoured regiments who liberated our towns and villages in January 1945 during the Ardennes Offensive.'

Turret Specifications	
Main armament:	QF 17pdr
Additional weapons:	.30cal Browning MG M1919A4 coaxial .50cal Browning MG HB M2 flexible AA turret mount 2in smoke bomb thrower
Armour thickness gun shield:	3.5in (89mm)
Armour thickness mantlet:	1.5in (38mm)
Armour thickness front:	3.0in (76mm)
Armour thickness sides:	2.0in (50mm)
Armour thickness rear:	2.5in (63mm)
Armour thickness top:	1.0in (25mm)

Chapter 4

M4A3(76)W Sherman Tank
Beffe

Location: Set your navigation device to Rue de l'Eglise 12, 6987 Rendeux, Belgium. This is a restaurant. The tank is opposite where Rue de l'Eglise meets a road called Sous-le-Tonan.

This M4A3(76)W Sherman tank, now on display in the village of Beffe, was part of the US Army, Company C, 771st Tank Battalion. On 8 January 1945, during a move from Magoster to Marcourai, the Sherman slipped on the icy road and slid into a ditch. As the tank was recovered out from the ditch, it hit a daisy chain of German mines that disabled the tank and set it on fire; the bogies were destroyed at the same time by the mines. Other parts of the tank that are missing were probably taken as spares by the US Army throughout the remainder of the war or by post-war tourists.

The driver, Salvatore Di Martino, was killed, and the commander, Leutenant Norbert E Karl, was severely wounded but survived the war. For many years, the Sherman was left abandoned beside the road between the villages of Magoster and Beffe, where it had been knocked out. It was very evocative of the Battle of the Bulge, as it was left at an angle in the middle of the fence with its turret pointing forward but slightly to its right, as if taking aim at an enemy tank. The co-drivers hatch had been buckled and jammed open since the day it was disabled.

In December 1984, the commander of the 3rd Armored Division, based in Germany, agreed to recover and restore the tank as a war memorial. After 40 years of resting in that field, it was recovered and deposited on the concrete base in the centre of Beffe. The rear engine deck hatches with torsion bars are not original; they were rescued from a 1950s M74 Tank Recovery Vehicle (TRV) range wreck and fitted during the 1980s restoration work.

The plaque on the tank's side is a dedication to the officers and men of US Army Task Force Hogan, (3rd Battalion, 33rd Armor 'Pickles', 3rd Armored Division). Between 22 and 25 December 1944, they were surrounded by German troops of Kampfgruppe Bayer and repulsed repeated attacks. After running out of fuel and ammunition, they destroyed their equipment and infiltrated enemy lines around Beffe and rejoined the bulk of the 3rd Armored Division.

Specifications	
Dimensions:	L: 24ft 9in (7.54m); W: 9ft 10in (2.99m); H: 9ft 9in (2.97m); Wt: 33.1 tons (33.65 tonnes)
Engine:	Ford GAA 8-cylinder, 4-cycle, petrol/gasoline 500hp engine
Crew:	5
Main armament:	76mm M1A1, M1A1C or M1A2 in mount M62 in turret
Additional weapons:	Two .30cal Browning MG M1919A4; .50cal Browning MG HB M2 AA mount; 2-inch Mortar M3 smoke bomb thrower
Armour thickness:	0.5in to 3.5in (12mm to 88.9mm)
Max. road speed:	26mph (41.8km/h)
Total built:	4,542

Chapter 5
Panther Ausf. G Tank
Grandmenil

Location: Set your navigation device to Manhay History 44 Museum, Voie Habotte 2, 6960 Manhay (Grandmenil), Belgium. The museum is by a roundabout. The Panther tank is by the side of the roundabout, between the Rue d'Erezée N807 and Rue Alphonse Poncelet.

On 24 December 1944, five German 2nd SS Das Reich Panther tanks were damaged as they advanced through a minefield between Manhay and Grandmenil. Those that could not be repaired were abandoned by their crews. The Panther tank on display at the Grandmenil roundabout was one of those Panthers. The turret number, 407, is not believed to be correct.

The Panther tank column had been driving west along the N807 Route d'Erezée from Manhay. Two 90mm GMC M36 tank destroyers of Company B, 628th Tank Destroyer Battalion were lying in wait 150m northeast of the Grandmenil roundabout (which was a crossroad junction in 1944) in the Rue Alphonese Poncelet. One Panther was knocked out when it was hit in the side by an M36 tank destroyer 90mm armour-piercing shell. A second Panther returned fire, and the lead M36 blew up in a tremendous explosion as it was trying to back away. The second M36 fired at the front armour of another Panther, but the shell failed to penetrate. That Panther tank commander spotted the second American M36 near some trees, fired and disabled it.

Two Panthers further down the road column had problems and blocked the road, and one tank commander was seriously injured in the head. Another tank had to be towed after it slipped off the road trying to get around the stationary Panthers. These road blockages and the fighting at the Grandmenil roundabout may have been the reason for the remaining tanks driving into the fields. The US 238th Engineer Combat Battalion had laid mines in the fields on both sides of the road just before the Grandmenil roundabout. They could not be seen by the German tank crews as there had been a fresh coating of snow overnight. (This tank battle was researched by Bob Konings. To read a more detailed account, go to www.grandmenil.com)

There are plans for this PzKpfw V Ausf. G Panther to be repainted and moved to the other side of the road next to the Manhay History 44 Museum (MHM44) and exhibited in a roofed, but open-air, structure.

Specifications	
Dimensions:	L: 29ft (8.86m); W: 11ft 2in (3.42m); H: 10ft 2in (3.10m); Wt: 44.78 tons (45.5 tonnes)
Engine:	Maybach HL 230 P30 V12, water-cooled, 600hp petrol/gasoline engine
Crew:	5
Main armament:	7.5cm Kw.K.42 L/70, 82 rounds
Additional weapons:	Two 7.92mm M.G.34 machine guns
Armour thickness:	0.6in to 3in (16mm to 80mm); (Turret front and mantlet 4in/4.3in or 100mm to 110mm)
Max. road speed:	28.5mph (46km/h)
Total built:	2961 approx.

Chapter 6
M4A1(76)W Sherman Tank
La Roche-en-Ardenne

Location: Set your navigation device to Rue du Presbytére 4-6, 6980 La Roche-en-Ardenne, Belgium. It is in the car park near the river at the junction with Quai de l'Ourthe N89.

On 11 January 1945, at around midday, after getting the 'all clear' from the mine disposal team, British armoured reconnaissance vehicles of 2nd Derbyshire Yeomanry Regiment, 51st Highland Division, entered the bombed remains of the German-occupied La Roche-en-Ardenne. They were supported by armoured vehicles of the 1st Northamptonshire Yeomanry Regiment. On 12 January 1945, British units linked up with an armoured reconnaissance patrol from the US 84th Division. This tank is dedicated to the American soldiers who helped the British to liberate the town from German forces.

However, despite this dedication, this tank did not take part in the liberation of the town. It was given the name 'Amboy' by its crew and has the hull number 3904. M4A1 Sherman tanks armed with the 76mm gun had not taken part in D-Day, although a few made their combat debut in Normandy in late July 1944.

After World War Two, the tank was used as a 'hard target' on the Belgian Army live firing range at Camp Lagland, near Arlon. It was rescued from certain destruction and put on display at the 40–45 Memories Musée in Awaille, Belgium. In 2004, following the museum's closure, the Sherman was transported to the picturesque town of La Roche-en-Ardenne to be used as a war memorial by the River Ourthe.

It replaced an M26 Pershing tank that was on the same spot. Pershing tanks only saw action in the last months of the war in 1945 and did not play a part in the Battle of the Bulge. The town council felt that an M4A1(76)W Sherman tank was more representative of the type of Allied tanks that were used to liberate the local area and the town of La Roche-en-Ardenne. The M26 Pershing went to Le Camp Roi Albert in Marche.

There is a lot of visible damage to the Sherman, which some associate with combat during World War Two, however, it should be remembered that this tank was recovered from an Army firing range. Most of the holes and cracks in the armour are visible on the front glacis plate and near the driver's hatch under the turret.

Specifications	
Dimensions:	L: 24ft 6in (7.46m); W: 8ft 9in (2.66m); H: 9ft 9in (2.97m); Wt: 31.5 tons (32 tonnes)
Engine:	Continental R975 C4 9-cylinder, 4-cycle, radial petrol/gasoline 460hp engine
Crew:	5
Main armament:	76mm M1A1, M1A1C or M1A2 in mount M62 in turret
Additional weapons:	Two .30cal Browning MG M1919A4; .5cal Browning MG HB M2 AA mount; 2-inch Mortar M3 smoke bomb thrower
Armour thickness:	0.5in to 3.5in (12mm to 88.9mm)
Max. road speed:	21mph (33.79km/h)
Total built:	3,426

Chapter 7

M10 17pdr SP Achilles IIC
La Roche-en-Ardenne

Location: Set your navigation device to Rue du Chalet 61, 6980 La Roche-en-Ardenne, Belgium. This is a hotel called Le Chalet. It is by the junction with the Avenue du Hadja, opposite the M10 17pdr SP Achilles IIC.

The British 51st Highland Division was given the task of opening the road to, and the subsequent capture of, the attractive town of La Roche-en-Ardenne on the River Ourthe. On 11 January 1945, at around midday, after getting the 'all clear' from the mine disposal team, armoured reconnaissance vehicles of 2nd Derbyshire Yeomanry Regiment entered the bombed remains of the town. They were supported by armoured vehicles of the 1st Northamptonshire Yeomanry Regiment and the infantry of The Black Watch, 51st Highland Division. Once the last German troops had been dealt with, the streets were cleared of debris. This enabled other regiments to cross the river and continue the advance south towards the village of Ortho. On 12 January 1945, British units linked up with an armoured reconnaissance patrol from the US 84th Infantry Division.

The QF 17pdr anti-tank gun was the main gun mounted inside the open turret of this M10 17pdr SP Achilles IIC. The weapon was originally designed as a field gun, and it performed so well in North Africa that the engineers back in Britain came up with the idea of putting it in the new Lend-Lease, 3-inch GMC M10 tank destroyer. The problem with the original M10 was that it used American manufactured 75mm ammunition, and the D-Day planners predicted a supply issue. The American guns were taken out and replaced with these British-made guns in 1,100 vehicles.

They were given the designation 'M10 17pdr SP Achilles IIC.' The British Army did not use the American term 'tank destroyer', preferring the term 'self-propelled gun (SP).' Self-propelled anti-tank guns were given names starting with the letter 'A', like Archer, Alecto, Avenger and Achilles. They had thin armour and an open-topped turret. They were faster than the more heavily armoured Sherman and Churchill tanks. Tactically, they were not designed to be at the spearhead of an armoured assault. Their crews were trained to protect the flanks of an assault from counterattack by finding locations with good fields of vision and ambushing the enemy from camouflaged locations at long range.

Specifications	
Dimensions:	L: 23ft 10in (7.27m); W: 10ft (3.04m); H over AA gun: 9ft 6in (2.89m); Wt: 29.10 tons (29.57 tonnes)
Engine:	General Motors 6046 12-cylinder, 2-cycle, twin in-line diesel 410hp engine
Crew:	5
Main armament:	QF 17pdr in turret mount No.3 Mk.1 in turret
Additional weapons:	.50cal MG HB M2 AA mount on turret; 2-inch muzzle loading mortar
Armour thickness:	0.375in to 2.25in (9.5mm to 57mm)
Max. road speed:	30mph (48.2km/h)
Total built:	Achilles = 1,100, M10 = 4.993, M10A1 = 1,713

Chapter 8
Jagdpanzer 38 (G13 Hetzer)
La Roche-en-Ardenne

Location: Set your navigation device to Rue du Presbytére 4-6, 6980 La Roche-en-Ardenne, Belgium. It is a car park near the river at the junction with Quai de l'Ourthe N89, which contains the M4A1(76)W Sherman of Chapter 6. From here, you have to walk a few metres to the Musée de la Bataille des Ardennes, Rue Chamont 5.

The Jagdpanzer 38 was quick to build and cheap compared with the cost of constructing a Tiger, Tiger II or Panther tank. It was mechanically reliable, easily concealed, hard-hitting and, when used right, a hard to kill vehicle. A company or platoon of Jagdpanzer 38 tank destroyers working together, concealed in a good location, could damage or knockout a considerable number of attacking enemy tanks. It was only 2.10m (6ft 10.6in) high. This was ideal for ambush tactics. It was armed with a powerful high-velocity 7.5cm Pak 39 L/48 long-range gun that could knockout most Allied tanks. The Jagdpanzer 38 was not officially called the Hetzer during World War Two.

It was not designed to be a close combat vehicle used at the head of an attack like a tank. It was instead a self-propelled anti-tank gun that was intended to be deployed on the flanks to stop counterattacks. A pack of Jagdpanzer 38 tank hunters would hide in a wood or thick hedgerow and pick off enemy tanks at long range. The sloping front armour gave the crew reasonable protection from frontal attack and, so long as the driver pointed the front of the vehicle at any threat, the crew would typically survive a hit from an armour-piercing enemy shell. The thin armour on the sides of the vehicle and at the rear meant that there was a risk of being knocked out by flank and rear attacks with armour-piercing shells. If there was a danger of being outflanked, the driver had to change to a different location quickly.

In 1944, the relatively reliable Panzer 38(t) tank was considered outclassed and obsolete, and it had been withdrawn from frontline units. The Jagdpanzer 38 utilised the tried and tested components of the Panzer 38(t) tank on a new wider hull. After the war, the Swiss government ordered some Jagdpanzer 38 tank hunters to equip their army. The first ten that they received were German specification Jagdpanzer 38 tank hunters. The rest were new-build vehicles for the Swiss G13 contract. This tank is a Swiss Army G13 Jagdpanzer 38.

Specifications	
Dimensions:	L: 20ft 7in (6.27m); W: 8ft 7in (2.63m); H: 6ft 10.6in (2.10m); Wt: 15.74 tons (16 tonnes)
Engine:	Praga EPA AC 2800 6-cylinder, petrol/gasoline 160hp
Crew:	4
Main armament:	7.5cm Pak 39 L/48
Additional weapons:	7.92mm M.G.34
Armour thickness:	0.4in to 2.4in (10mm to 60mm)
Max. road speed:	24.8mph (40km/h)
Total built:	2,612

Chapter 9

M4 Sherman Tank
Wibrin

Location: Set your navigation device to Rue du Tilleul 15, 6666 Houffalize (Wibrin), Belgium. It is by the side of the road, in front of the Eglise de Wibrin church, at the junction of Rue du Bourg and Rue du Tilleul.

German Panther tank crew member Hans Herost, of the 116th Panzer Division, recorded his memories of his unit's encounter with six Allied M4 Sherman tanks in the village of Wilbrin on 14 January 1945. 'We did not take the streets but drove across the fields and meadows because of all the mines. We were on the hill about 1,000m away from the village church. From up there, we saw the Sherman tank that is now the war memorial in Wilbrin. It was in the same place on that day. This tank, with its small gun, was barely a threat to us. The Panther tank that was next to me shot at the enemy tank. The shell hit the sloping front armour and bounced off. You can still see the deep gouge on the front. It bounced upwards and hit the Sherman's gun, damaging it. When the American crew fired, the tube burst. You can see the damage it caused today. The second shell hit the big bolts on the bottom of the front armour and again bounced off. The third hit went through the armour, and it caught fire.'

Lieutenant von Elterlein in Panther 706 wrote: 'All of a sudden, six American tanks showed up in front of us! Both Pz. Vs immediately shot and destroyed four of them. Two Shermans, with infantry riding on top, tried to overrun my position under the cover of a "hollow road". Within 3 minutes, my gunner destroyed both Shermans at close range.'

The local priest saved the tank from scrap metal merchants, who had already cut away some of the rear and right side of the tank. It was decided to make it the village's war memorial. The tank belonged to the US Army Company G, 3rd Battalion, 66th Armored Regiment, Task Force B, 2nd Armored Division. The tanks supported troops from Company F, 41st Armored Infantry Regiment. The 66AR war diary records only four Sherman tanks lost and estimated the Germans had 12 tanks reinforced with anti-tank guns and a battalion of infantry. The additional welded spaced armour in front of the tank driver's position did not stop the Panther tank's 75mm round. It went straight through the plate and the hull armour. The information sign inside the turret is wrong. It is not an M4A3 Sherman, it is a late production M4.

Specifications	
Dimensions:	L: 19ft 4in (5.89m); W: 8ft 7in (2.61m); H: 9ft (2.74m); Wt: 29.86 tons (30.34 tonnes)
Engine:	Continental R975 C1 9-cylinder, 4-cycle, radial petrol/gasoline 400hp engine
Crew:	5
Main armament:	75mm gun M3 in mount M34A1 in turret
Additional weapons:	Two .30cal Browning MG M1919A4; .50cal Browning MG HB M2 AA mount; 2-inch Mortar M3 smoke bomb thrower
Armour thickness:	0.5in to 3.5in (12mm to 88.9mm)
Max. road speed:	21mph (33.79km/h)
Total built:	6,748

Chapter 10
Panther Ausf. G Tank
Houfflaize

Location: Set your navigation device to Rue Saint-Roch 1, 6660 Houffalize, Belgium.

On 18 December 1944, during the early part of the Battle of the Bulge, the Reconnaissance Battalion of the 116th Panzer Division overpowered American resistance south of the village of Houfflaize, near the Luxembourg border. They wanted to capture the strategically important bridges over the River Ourthe before they could be blown up. Problems over the supply of fuel and traffic jams on the roads around Dasburg were causing delays for the main advance. By the evening, the division was ready to thrust westwards towards Houfflaize. The town was taken without a fight. Between 20 December 1944 and 16 January 1945, Houfflaize stayed in German control. Allied bombers targeted Houfflaize many times to try and disrupt their supply chain. Unfortunately, 189 Belgium civilians were killed in the bombing, and around 350 houses were destroyed or damaged, devastating the town. The First and Third American armies were trying to encircle the retreating Germans in a pincer movement. On 16 January 1945, they linked up at Houfflaize, but the bulk of the threatened German units managed to escape the trap.

The Houfflaize Panther Ausf. G tank, turret number 111, initially saw service with the 1st Battalion, 24th Panzer Regiment in Normandy in the summer of 1944. It managed to escape destruction and capture in the Falaise pocket. In November 1945, it was transferred to the 1st Battalion, 16th Panzer Regiment, which was part of the 116th Panzer Division. This tank was the 17th Panther Ausf. G tank to leave the factory gates of the Daimler-Benz Plant 40 factory in Berlin.

As the tank was being driven over the narrow river bridge, the driver steered too far to the right. It toppled off the bridge and landed upside down on its turret. Other, incorrect, accounts suggest a bomb blast threw this 45.5-tonne tank into the river Ourthe. There were no tank recovery vehicles available, so the Germans abandoned it in the river. The remains of the crew were discovered when the Panther was pulled from the river. It was repainted with a three-tone camouflage scheme and displayed with the 'Windhund' insignia of the 116th Panzer Division. The turret number, 401, is wrong. The correct number was III.

On 3 May 2017, the Panther was moved to Bastogne Barracks for restoration work in partnership with the Krings Collection and Panzer Farm. The town has plans to erect a cover over the tank when it returns.

Specifications	
Dimensions:	L: 29ft (8.86m); W: 11ft 2in (3.42m); H: 10ft 2in (3.10m); Wt: 44.78 tons (45.5 tonnes)
Engine:	Maybach HL 230 P30 V12, water-cooled, 600hp petrol/gasoline engine
Crew:	5
Main armament:	7.5cm Kw.K.42 L/70, 82 rounds
Additional weapons:	Two 7.92mm M.G.34 machine guns
Armour thickness:	0.6in to 3in (16mm to 80mm); (Turret front and mantlet 4in to 4.3in or 100mm to 110mm)
Max. road speed:	28.5mph (46km/h)
Total built:	2961 approx.

Chapter 11
M4A1(76)W Sherman Tank
Vielsalm

Location: Set your navigation device to Rue Hermanmont 3, 6690 Vielsalm, Belgium. This is an Aldi store. The tank can be found a few metres away on the other south side of the road, by the junction with Rue Jules Bary and Rue Hermanmont N675.

US Army General Bruce Clarke offered a Sherman tank to the town of Vielsalm in 1976. It was transported to its present location from the Grafenwohr Depot in Germany and arrived on 20 February 1984. It was dedicated to the memory of every American unit that fought in the Saint Vith salient during the Battle of the Bulge.

Notice this M4A1(76)W Sherman has the bigger 76mm gun with a one-piece cast nose gun mantlet. It has a cast hull and the larger T23 type turret. The additional protective armour plating for the driver and hull machine gunner found on many other Sherman tanks has not been welded onto this hull. The suspension is the early VVSS type. It has a hull number of 4953 and was constructed around August 1944.

The number 7, followed by a triangle, on the front of the tank hull is the tactical marking for the US Army 7th Armored Division. The number 40, followed by a triangle, is the abbreviation for the 40th Tank Battalion. The capital letter 'B', followed by the number 4, indicates that this tank was part of Company B (or 'Baker') as tank number 4.

The town of Vielsalm contained one of two strategically important bridges over the River Salm. The other was further south in nearby Salmchâteau. The 7th Armored Division defended an area between Vielsalm and the important crossroad town of St Vith, 13 miles to the east. The plaque on the tank reads, 'The American 7th Armored Division and attached units headquartered in Vielsalm during the crucial period of the German offensive of the Ardennes in 1944 held the important centre of St Vith preventing any advance and any exploitation of this main line, thus frustrating the German offensive by its sacrifice permitting the launching of the Allied counter-offensive. 17–23 December 1944. Dedicated 9 June 1984.'

Specifications	
Dimensions:	L: 24ft 6in (7.46m); W: 8ft 9in (2.66m); H: 9ft 9in (2.97m); Wt: 31.5 tons (32 tonnes)
Engine:	Continental R975 C4 9-cylinder, 4-cycle, radial petrol/gasoline 460hp engine
Crew:	5
Main armament:	76mm M1A1, M1A1C or M1A2 in mount; M62 in turret
Additional weapons:	Two .30cal Browning MG M1919A4; .50cal Browning MG HB M2 AA mount; 2-inch Mortar M3 smoke bomb thrower
Armour thickness:	0.5in to 3.5in (12mm to 88.9mm)
Max. road speed:	21mph (33.79km/h)
Total built:	3,426

Chapter 12

Tiger II Tank
La Gleize

Location: Set your navigation device to Rue de l'Eglise, 4987 Stoumont (La Gleize), Belgium. This is the December 44 Museum – Battle of the Bulge. The Tiger II tank is opposite the entrance by the church.

The official designation of this tank was Panzerkampfwagen Tiger Ausf. B (Sd.Kfz.182). It was also called the Königstiger, the German name for the Bengal tiger, but it is often incorrectly translated as the Royal Tiger or the more popular version, King Tiger. It is also called the Tiger II.

It has the number 213 on the side of the turret. It was the platoon command tank of SS-Obersturmführer Dollinger and was part of the Kampfgruppe Peiper. Tank 213 and another Tiger II, turret number 221, plus a Panzer IV tank were defending the Werimont Farm high ground on the outskirts of La Gleize. On 21 December 1944, over 20 US tanks of Task Force McGeorge and Task Force Lovelady of the 3rd Armored Division attacked La Gleize from the direction of Roanne-Coo. Tanks of the US 740th Tank Battalion in Stoumont bombarded La Gleize with high explosive shells. Tiger II 213 tank's main gun was hit and the front third of the barrel was blown off. The gun could no longer be fired, so the tank had to be abandoned.

In the summer of 1945, Tiger II 213 was purchased for a bottle of cognac from the American Army battlefield salvage unit by Madame Jenny Geenen-Dewez, the owner of a local inn, La Fermette, thus saving it for posterity. In 1951, the restoration of the tank started. The 88mm gun was repaired by welding it to part of an original Panther tank 75mm barrel found in Falize, Malmedy. In 1994, the damaged and missing front, side and rear track mudguards were rebuilt.

Although many tools and components are missing from the tank, it is still in reasonably good shape. The pistol port plug is missing from the large, heavy hatch at the rear of the turret. This access hatch was used to load ammunition and as an escape hatch. There is evidence of shrapnel or small-arms fire on the underneath of the gun mantlet. The Losterkennungstafel (poison gas indicator) cardholder brackets are still visible; one is on top of the gun mantlet, and the other two are on top of the turret roof. The damage to the glacis plate may have happened after its capture.

Specifications	
Dimensions:	L: 33ft 9in (10.28m); W: 12ft 4in (3.75m); H: 10ft 2in (3.09m); Wt: 68.69 tons (69.80 tonnes)
Engine:	Maybach HL 230 P30, 12-cylinder, 750hp engine
Crew:	5
Main armament:	8.8cm Kw.K.43 L/71
Additional weapons:	3x 7.92mm M.G.34 or M.G.42
Armour thickness:	1in to 7.3in (25mm to 185mm)
Max. road speed:	23.6mph (38km/h)
Total built:	489

Chapter 13
Sherman VC Firefly Tank
Thimister-Clermont

Location: Set your navigation device to Les Béolles 4, 4890 Thimister-Clermont, Belgium. The tank is outside the Remember Museum 39–45, which is part of a farm complex.

The sign next to this tank declares that this Sherman tank is an M4A4. This is not the correct designation. The hull was built as an M4A4 but converted to a British Sherman VC Firefly tank. The hull was retrieved from the Belgian Army Camp Elsenborn, near Liège, in 1998. The Firefly turret has been replaced with a standard Sherman tank turret with a short-barrelled 75mm M3 gun. The Firefly turret was larger and mounted the powerful QF 17pdr gun. The right side of the front glacis plate does not have a hull-mounted machine gun, as Firefly tanks had this removed and blanked over to enable more 17pdr ammunition to be stored. British Sherman VC Firefly 17pdr tanks saw action in the Battle of the Bulge. They were normally deployed in a troop of four tanks: three Shermans armed with a 75mm gun and one Sherman Firefly to deal with heavily armoured German Panther and Tiger tanks.

On 11 September 1944, the area around Thimister-Clermont was liberated by US Army troops. The farm buildings were used as a billet by 110 soldiers from the US 1st Infantry Division. The Remember Museum 1939–45 founder, Marcel Schmetz, was an 11-year-old boy when the Americans arrived. He lived on the farm during the German occupation of Belgium. There had been shortages and restrictions and he remembers having a fantastic time with the American troops as they shared their rations, sweets and chocolates with the farmer and the children.

When news of the surprise German attack on 16 December 1944 in the Ardennes was received, they had to leave very quickly to join the counter-attack. The men, expecting to return, left a lot of equipment at the farm. Marcel's family stored all the American soldiers' personal items in one of their farmyard barns. The soldiers never returned to collect it. Many things were left behind by the GIs in the rush to get going and are now some of the items on display in the museum. The Germans did not manage to reach as far as Thimister-Clermont during the Battle of the Bulge. A replica wooden 3-inch GMC M10 tank destroyer is exhibited inside the museum. Check the museum's website for opening times before you start your journey: www.remembermuseum.be/en

Specifications	
Dimensions:	L: 25ft 9in (7.84m); W: 8ft 9in (2.66m); H: 9ft (2.74m); Wt: 72,100lb (32.1 tons to 32.7 tonnes)
Engine:	Chrysler A57 30-cylinder, 4-cycle, multibank, Petrol/gasoline 425hp engine
Crew:	4
Current turret main armament:	75mm M3 gun with M34A1 mantlet
Original Firefly turret main armament:	QF 17pdr gun
Additional weapons:	.30cal Browning MG M1919A4 coaxial; .50cal Browning MG HB M2 flexible AA turret mount
Armour thickness:	0.5in to 3.5in (12.7mm to 88.9mm)
Max. road speed:	25mph (40.23km/h)
Total built:	Over 2,000

Chapter 14

Turrets
Bastogne Encirclement Route

Roads that lead into the centre of Bastogne in the Ardennes have World War Two Sherman Tank turrets positioned at the frontline positions held between the US and German forces in the Battle of the Bulge. They symbolically indicate the December 1944 perimeter of the encirclement of Bastogne.

The thickly armoured Sherman Jumbo tank, nicknamed 'Cobra King', was commanded by Lieutenant Charles Boggess. On 26 December 1944, this tank was the first spearhead of the armour and infantry column that smashed through the German front line and liberated the siege of Bastogne. It was the 'First in Bastogne'.

Tank Turret No 1

This M4(76) Sherman tank turret can be found in the Rue de Neufchateau N85, Bastogne, Belgium. It is a memorial to GI Lieutenant Ernest Glessener, the first Allied soldier killed at Bastogne. On 10 September 1944, he was killed near this spot just after he had destroyed a German tank. It is a T23 turret with a 76mm gun and can be identified by the lack of a thread on the barrel and the presence of the gun mantlet. There are still the remains of the 10th Armored Divisional patch on the right side of the turret near the hedge. The following numbers can be seen on the turret: D82081 and C192.

Tank Turret No 2

This M4(76) Sherman tank T23 turret is in the village of Champs, along the N854, northwest of Bastogne. This turret was initially positioned by the road to Marche, but it was later relocated to its present position in Champs. This turret has the numbers D82081 and C377.

Tank Turret No 3

This M4(75) Sherman tank D78461 high bustle turret is in Rue de La Roche N834 outside the Bastogne Barracks. Initially, there were two Sherman tank turrets positioned at this location: one on each side of the road. Now there is just one. The turret itself has a serial number 6510.

Tank Turret No 4

This M4A3 large hatch Sherman 75mm tank turret can be found on the road from Assenois to Bastogne, about 100 miles south of the junction of the Ru du Fortin and the Rue de la Fagne D'hi by the Bastogne industrial park. It is set on a concrete plinth next to a fortified pillbox. It used to be positioned in the Rue de La Roche N834 outside the Bastogne Barracks (near to Tank Turret No 3) but was moved to this location in December 2020 after being restored. (Fabrice Gérardy)

Tank Turret No 5

This M4(76) Sherman tank T23 turret is in the village car park of Mageret, Rue de Clervaux N874, northeast of Bastogne in Belgium. Like No 2, this Sherman tank turret has also moved from its original position by the N30 to its present location in Mageret. The turret shows the numbers D82081 and C367.

Tank Turret No 6

This M4(76) Sherman tank T23 turret is on Rue Gustave Delperdange N874 in Bastogne and can be seen on the left of the road as you drive towards the Mardasson War Memorial and Bastogne War Museum. It has the patch of the 10th Armored Division on its right side. On its left side, in the bottom corner on the right below the American star, there is a hole from a direct hit. There is a thread on the barrel for its counterweight, the gun mantlet is still in its position, and the serial number, LO-447S278, is on the turret.

Tank Turret No 7

This M4(75) Sherman tank D78461 high bustle turret is in the village of Marvie, along the Rue de La Californie, southeast of Bastogne. If you look at the front view, you see to the left of the gun a hole from a direct hit. To the right of the gun, there is another hole in the turret armour from another direct hit. The tank turret carries the casting number 6352.

Tank Turret No 8

This M4(76) Sherman tank T23 turret can be found in the Rue de la Chappelle N30, Bastogne. It is missing its muzzle breech, but you can still see the screw thread at the end of the gun barrel.

Tank Turret No 9

This M4(75) Sherman tank D78461 high bustle turret can be found in the Rue de Wiltz N84, east of Bastogne. This turret has the casting number 6605 and has no direct hit damage. It is positioned, coming from Bastogne, on the left-hand side of the road.

Tank Turret No 10

An M4 Sherman Firefly tank turret sits on top of a tree trunk at the entrance of the private drive that leads to the Château d'Isle-la-Hesse, the 1944 Battle of the Bulge headquarters of the US Army 101st Airborne Division. To find the turret, drive down to the end of the attractive tree lined road called Isle-la-Hesse. It was here that the 'Nuts!' reply to the German request that the Americans in Bastogne surrender was typed. This turret used to be on display in the centre of Bastogne.

Chapter 15

Jagdpanzer 38 (G13 Hetzer)
Bastogne War Museum

Location: Set your navigation device to Bastogne War Museum, Colline du Mardasson 5, 6600 Bastogne, Belgium. It is near the junction of Rue de Clervaux, at the junction with Route de Bizory. Follow signs for the Bastogne War Museum and the Mémorial du Mardasson.

This Jagdpanzer 38 did not take part in the Battle of the Bulge. It was built after the war for the Swiss Army. Those built during World War Two were not officially called the Hetzer. The German Jagdpanzer 38 tank hunters were assigned to Heeres Panzerjäger Abteilungen (Army Tank Hunter Battalions). They did take part in the Battle of the Bulge.

They were not intended to be used as a tank at the front of an attack in a major offensive. The Jagdpanzer 38 was an ambush weapon. They would hunt in packs on the flank of any major attack in a location that had good long-range visibility. They would stay concealed until they spotted enemy units trying a flanking attack. They also provided infantry regiments with a mobile anti-tank destroyer resource.

Notice how the front glacis plate and the lower front hull armour plate are welded and interlocked together. This form of connection was proven to provide extra strength to a joint. The Jagdpanzer 38 upper glacis plate was 60mm thick and sloped at 30° from the horizontal. The lower front hull plate was also 60mm thick but angled at 50°. The lower hull side armour was 20mm thick and sloped inwards at an angle of 75°. The rear armour was 20mm thick angled at 75°. The roof armour was 10mm thick. The belly armour was 8mm thick. The Schürzen side skirt armour was made from 5mm-thick steel plate. It was designed to protect the 20mm thick lower side hull armour from the Soviet 14.5mm anti-tank rifle.

Overall, the vehicle was successful. It was quick to build and cheap compared with the cost of constructing a Tiger, King Tiger or Panther tank. It was mechanically reliable, easily concealed, hard-hitting, and when used right, a hard to kill vehicle. A company or platoon of Jagdpanzer 38 tank destroyers working together, concealed in a good location, could damage or knockout a considerable number of attacking enemy tanks.

Specifications	
Dimensions:	L: 20ft 7in (6.27m); W: 8ft 7in (2.63m); H: 6ft 11in (2.10m); Wt: 15.74 tons (16 tonnes)
Engine:	Praga EPA AC 2800, 6-cylinder, petrol/gasoline 160hp
Crew:	4
Main armament:	7.5cm Pak 39 L/48
Additional weapons:	7.92mm M.G.34 machine gun
Armour thickness:	0.3in to 2.4in (8mm to 60mm)
Max. road speed:	24.8mph (40km/h)
Total built:	2,612

Chapter 16
Sherman VC Firefly Tank
Bastogne War Museum

Location: Set your navigation device to Bastogne War Museum, Colline du Mardasson 5, 6600 Bastogne, Belgium. It is near the junction of Rue de Clervaux at the junction with Route de Bizory. Follow signs for the Bastogne War Museum and the Mémorial du Mardasson.

The post-war Belgian Army was equipped with many different World War Two tanks. When these were replaced with more modern vehicles, some were used for target practice on live firing ranges. That was the fate of this tank. The damage seen on this Sherman VC Firefly hull, including the large hole on the right side of the tank, was inflicted by Cold War ammunition. The museum did not repair the damage, as it gave the tank a dramatic appearance: as if it had been knocked out in the heavy fighting around Bastogne during the Battle of the Bulge. The serial number, 3022791, painted on the side of the tank belonged to an M4 Sherman tank constructed by Baldwin Locomotive Works, not this tank. It is marked as a tank belonging to the US Army 2nd Battalion, 9th Armored Division, but they did not operate Sherman Firefly tanks.

The British upgraded American-built M4A4 Sherman tanks, sent to them under the Lend-Lease scheme, by mounting the powerful 17pdr anti-tank gun in an altered turret. They were given the designation Sherman VC Firefly. To make room for additional 17pdr ammunition, the Firefly hull machine gun was removed, and a piece of armour was welded over the top. After World War Two, the Belgian Army refitted a ball machine gun mount in the hull on some of their VC Firefly tanks, and this is what happened to this example. At the back of the tank, you can see the weld marks from where the gun lock used to be and the two fire extinguisher holders. The brackets for the Firefly's rear stowage box are also present. These fixtures were not normally fitted on M4A4 Sherman tanks armed with the standard 75mm gun and can be used to help identify this tank as a British converted Firefly. Inside the tank, you can see the remains of the 17pdr gun cradle. The tank's turret is missing, and it has been replaced with a Sherman turret fitted with a 75mm gun from a different tank. The original turret may have been heavily damaged or removed prior to the hull being placed out on the firing range. Firefly tanks saw combat with British and Commonwealth forces in the Ardennes during the Battle of the Bulge.

Specifications	
Dimensions:	L: 25ft 9in (7.84m); W: 8ft 9in (2.66m); H: 9ft (2.74m); Wt: 31.29 tons (31.79 tonnes)
Engine:	Chrysler A57 30-cylinder, 4-cycle, multibank petrol/gasoline 425hp engine
Crew:	4 (commander, driver, gunner, loader)
Current turret main armament:	75mm M3 gun with M34A1 mantlet
Main armament:	QF 17pdr anti-tank gun
Additional weapons:	Roof: .50cal Browning MG HB M2; Coaxial: .30cal Browning MG M1919A4; 2in bomb thrower fixed in turret
Armour thickness:	0.5in to 3.5in (12.7mm to 88.9mm)
Max. road speed:	25mph (40.23km/h)
Total built:	Over 2,000

Chapter 17
M4(105) Sherman Tank
Bastogne War Museum

Location: Set your navigation device to Bastogne War Museum, Colline du Mardasson 5, 6600 Bastogne, Belgium. It is near the junction of Rue de Clervaux at the junction with Route de Bizory. Follow signs for the Bastogne War Museum and the Mémorial du Mardasson.

This M4(105) Sherman tank has serial number 57304 and was built in June 1944. It was donated to the City of Bastogne by Lieutenant General William Robertson Desobry. He was a Major in the 10th US Armored Division when he was seriously injured at Noville on 19 December 1944 during the Battle of the Bulge. He commanded a task force known as 'Team Desobry', which held the road between Noville and Bourcy during the siege of Bastogne. It was renamed Rue de Général Desobry in his honour. His military ambulance was captured by the Germans, and he received treatment in one of their hospitals. He ended the war in Germany as a prisoner of war. When he was freed, he returned to the US Army and took part in the Allied occupation of Austria. During the Vietnam War, he served in the Mekong Delta. He retired as a three-star Lieutenant General in 1975.

The M4(105) Sherman tanks saw service in the Ardennes. It was normally deployed in a six-tank assault gun platoon. They were not designed to take on enemy tanks at close quarters, but they did carry a couple of high explosive anti-tank (HEAT) rounds for self-defence if they were surprised by enemy tanks. M4(105) Shermans provided close support to infantry and tank units when attacking concrete pillboxes, fortified farmhouses, soft-skinned lightly armoured vehicles, infantry concentrations and artillery batteries. It could fire a more powerful high explosive shell than Sherman tanks armed with a 75mm gun. The 105mm howitzer had an extra 10 degrees of elevation compared to the standard 75mm gun. They were designed to be fired as a static artillery howitzer and not on the move.

Unlike open-topped M7 Priest self-propelled artillery guns, the M4(105) Sherman gunner, loader and commander worked in a fully armoured enclosed turret. This meant the vehicle could work in an urban environment and get close to fortified strongpoints without fear of grenades being thrown into the fighting compartment and snipers firing from the upper levels of buildings. M4(105) Shermans were not issued with wet ammunition stowage racks, and instead they received armoured ammunition racks that could carry 66 105mm HE shells.

Specifications	
Dimensions:	L: 20ft 4in (5.89m); W: 8ft 9in (2.61m); H: 9ft 7in (2.74m); Wt: 30.98 tons (31.47 tonnes)
Engine:	Continental R975 C4 9-cylinder, 4-cycle, radial petrol/gasoline 400hp engine
Crew:	5
Main armament:	105mm howitzer M4 in mount M52 in turret
Additional weapons:	Two .30cal Browning MG M1919A4; .50cal Browning MG HB M2 AA mount; 2-inch Mortar M3 smoke bomb thrower
Armour thickness:	0.5in to 3.6in (12.7mm to 91.44mm)
Max. road speed:	21mph (33.79km/h)
Total built:	75

Chapter 18

M4A3E2(75) Sherman Jumbo Tank
Bastogne Barracks

Location: Set your navigation device to Bastogne Barracks, Rue de La-Roche 40, 6600 Bastogne, Belgium.

After World War Two, a large, heavily armoured Sherman M4A3E2(75) Jumbo tank was offered to dentist Dr Paul Michel, for use as a war memorial at Hermeton-sur-Meuse. He had helped save lives by turning his house into a medical centre. It was positioned by the side of the road with its gun pointing towards the other side of the trees across the River Meuse, as if waiting for German tanks to appear on the other bank. When the doctor died, the heirs of his estate claimed the Jumbo tank as their own. The ownership of the tank was investigated. It was discovered that the US Army still owned the tank. The US government started negotiations to get it shipped back to America, because it was rare and worth a lot of money. They were not happy that it was just left by the side of the road as a war memorial. After a year of talking, a deal was agreed: the Jumbo would stay in Belgium, and it would be restored to a working condition at the Bastogne Barracks Vehicle Restoration Centre and displayed at the Royal Museum of Armed Forces and Military History in Brussels. It was temporarily held at the depot of the Royal Museum of the Armed Forces in Landen, Belgium, but later moved to the Bastogne Barracks tank hall. Its serial number is 50511 and it was built in July 1944. Its correct registration number is 3083108.

To help tell the story of the first tank, nicknamed 'Cobra King', to break the siege of Bastogne, this Sherman M4A3E2(75) Jumbo tank has been painted to resemble its markings. Cobra King was part of General George S Patton's 3rd Army. The original Cobra King was shipped back from Vilseck in Germany to the US and was restored to the condition and markings it had on 26 December 1944, the date the siege was broken. Its 76mm gun, which was installed on the tank in March 1945, was replaced with an M3 75mm gun given by Fort Benning's Jumbo. It is now on display at the National Museum of the United States Army in Fort Belvoir, Virginia, US.

Specifications	
Dimensions:	L: 20ft 6in (6.27m); W: 9ft 7in (2.93m); H: 9ft 8in (2.95m); Wt: 37.5 tons (38.1 tonnes)
Engine:	Ford GAA 8-cylinder, 4-cycle, petrol/gasoline 500hp engine
Crew:	5
Main armament:	75mm gun M3 in mount T110 in turret
Additional weapons:	Two .30cal Browning MG M1919A4; .50cal Browning MG HB M2 AA mount; 2-inch Mortar M3 smoke bomb thrower
Armour thickness:	0.5in to 5.5in (12mm to 139.7mm)
Max. road speed:	22mph (35.4km/h)
Total built:	254

Chapter 19

Sherman VC Firefly Tanks
Bastogne Barracks

Location: Set your navigation device to Bastogne Barracks, Rue de La-Roche 40, 6600 Bastogne, Belgium.

Sherman Firefly tanks were used by British and Commonwealth forces in Belgium at the time of the Battle of the Bulge and later saw service in the Belgian Army. Bastogne Barracks has two Sherman VC 17pdr Firefly tanks. One has the hull serial number 5609 and displays the registration number T232568. It was built by Chrysler in October 1942. This tank was restored to a running condition by the Belgian Tank Museum volunteers and is now maintained by the Bastogne Barracks Vehicle Restoration Centre. The other has the hull serial number 16912 and was built by Chrysler in December 1942. Both were later modified by the British in order to mount the high-velocity QF 17pdr anti-tank gun. The latter of the two came from the Belgian Army Armour School in Leopoldsburg.

There were three variants of the Sherman Firefly in World War Two. The Sherman IC used a M4 hull. The Sherman Hybrid IC had a composite hull with a cast front and welded rear. The Sherman VC had a M4A4 hull. A small number were built for the US Army in April 1945 but did not see combat.

The 17pdr shells were much larger than those required for the standard Sherman tank 75mm gun. More space within the tank was required to store them. The solution to this problem was the removal of the hull machine gun. On this tank, you can see that there is no hull machine gun, and the hole has been blanked off. Extra appliqué armour was welded onto the exterior of the tank to add additional protection to the driver's position and ammunition stowage areas inside the tank.

In 1944, a troop of British Sherman tanks typically consisted of three Sherman tanks armed with the 75mm gun and one Sherman Firefly. The Firefly would have an 'oversight' role. The Sherman tanks 75mm high explosive shell was effective on soft-skinned targets, like enemy troops, machine gun nests, supply vehicles, artillery guns and towed anti-tank guns. Its armour piercing shells could knock out Panzer III and IV tanks but had problems dealing with the frontal armour of Tiger and Panther tanks. These targets would be dealt with by the Firefly. The long barrel was often camouflaged to make it look like a short-barrelled 75mm Sherman tank.

Specifications	
Dimensions:	L: 25ft 9in (7.84m); W: 8ft 9in (2.66m); H: 9ft (2.74m); Wt: 32.19 tons (32.71 tonnes)
Engine:	Chrysler A57 30-cylinder, 4-cycle, multibank, Petrol/gasoline 425hp engine
Crew:	4
Main armament	QF 17pdr anti-tank gun
Additional weapons:	Roof: .50cal Browning MG HB M2; Coaxial: .30cal Browning MG M1919A4; 2in smoke bomb thrower fixed in turret
Armour thickness:	0.5in to 3.5in (12.7mm to 88.9mm)
Max. road speed:	25mph (40km/h)
Total built:	Over 2,000

Chapter 20

M10 17pdr SP Achilles IIC
Bastogne Barracks

Location: Set your navigation device to Bastogne Barracks, Rue de La-Roche 40, 6600 Bastogne, Belgium.

The M10 17pdr SP Achilles IIC was a British variant of the American built 3-inch GMC M10 tank destroyer. There are two examples on display at Bastogne Barracks. It was armed with the QF 17pdr Mk.V high-velocity 76.2mm (3in) anti-tank gun. It replaced the M10 tank destroyer's less powerful 3-inch (76.2mm) Gun M7. The Mk.V version of the 17pdr was a modified version of the 17pdr Mk.II gun. The breech was equipped with two lugs to enable it to be fitted into the standard 3-inch (76.2mm) gun mount. The barrel was thinner, so a special collar, a circular piece of armour, was cast and welded over the gap around the barrel on the mantlet. It acted as a counterweight but was not enough to balance the long barrel of the 17pdr gun. An additional tubular counterweight was fitted to the gun barrel just behind the muzzle brake. The 17pdr anti-tank shells were much larger than those used on the standard 3-inch (76.2mm) gun. Ammunition stowage inside the M10 hull and turret had to be altered to accommodate the longer shells. Six shells could be carried in the ready racks in the turret. A further 44 shells were packed into the elongated hull ammunition racks.

Because of delays, the British only started the conversion work in April 1944. They had hoped to have had around 1,000 ready for D-Day, 6 June 1944, but only 124 had been altered by that date. After the invasion had started, the rate of conversions increased. They were issued to British Royal Artillery and Royal Canadian Artillery units. A total of 1,100 M10s were converted. While it is now commonly known by 'Achilles', this was not often used in official documents during World War Two. They were called 17pdr M10, or 17pdr SP M10, or even occasionally, 'Firefly'. Post-war, they saw service in the Belgian Army mechanised anti-tank battalions. The Belgian Army did refer to them as Achilles (Achille in French). The surviving Achilles on display came mostly from the Belgian Army training area at Camp Lagland near Arlon. The one on the trailer has early Belgian Army markings.

Specifications	
Dimensions:	L: 23ft 10in (7.27m); W: 10ft (3.04m); H over AA gun: 9ft 6in (2.89m); Wt: 29.10 tons (29.57 tonnes)
Engine:	General Motors 6046 12-cylinder, 2-cycle, twin in-line diesel 410hp engine
Crew:	5
Main armament:	QF 17pdr in turret mount; No.3 Mk.1 in turret
Additional weapons:	.50cal MG HB M2 AA mount on turret; 2-inch muzzle loading mortar
Armour thickness:	0.375in to 2.25in (9.5mm to 57mm)
Max. road speed:	30mph (48.2km/h)
Total built:	Achilles = 1,100, M10 = 4,993, M10A1 = 1,713

Chapter 21

M4A1(76)W Sherman Tank
Bastogne Barracks

Location: Set your navigation device to Bastogne Barracks, Rue de La-Roche 40, 6600 Bastogne, Belgium.

This Sherman tank was fitted with the longer, more powerful high-velocity 76mm gun, rather than the standard, shorter-barrelled 75mm gun that was mounted in the vast majority of Sherman tanks. Although they had arrived in England in early 1944, they were not used on D-Day. The US armoured divisions had spent most of their time familiarising themselves and training on Sherman tanks armed with the 75mm gun. It was felt that issuing a new type of Sherman tank would cause training and logistical problems as the new tank variant needed to be supplied with different ammunition.

After initial 'tank-on-tank' combat, reports were analysed by the US Army High Command in Europe, and it was quickly realised they needed a tank with a better gun. General Bradley ordered that the M4A1(76)W Sherman tanks being stored in England were to be shipped over to Normandy. They first saw combat in Operation *Cobra*, the American breakout from the beachheads, seven weeks after the D-Day landings. The 2nd and 3rd US Armored Divisions received approximately 60 M4A1(76)W Sherman tanks each. These would be evenly distributed amongst their tank units. M4A1(76)W Sherman tanks saw service in the Battle of the Bulge. They had larger cast metal turrets to cope with the longer 76mm gun than the M4A1(75) Sherman tanks, and to prevent damage to the gun on long journeys outside of a combat area, the barrel was clamped in an 'A' shaped gun lock, fitted on the front glacis plate.

In 1949, this tank was issued to the 2nd Lancers, the first post-war Belgian Army tank unit. It now displays the markings of the US 1st Army, 33rd Armour Regiment, 3rd Armored Division. At the time of the German attack during the Battle of the Bulge, the 3rd Armored Division were to the north of the advance. They received orders to head south and try to link up with General Patton's Third Army, which was fighting northwards. The number 30 painted on a yellow circle indicates that the tank cannot cross bridges that have a weight limit lower than 30 tons.

Specifications	
Dimensions:	L: 24ft 6in (7.46m); W: 8ft 9in (2.66m); H: 9ft 9in (2.97m); Wt: 31.5 tons (32 tonnes)
Engine:	Continental R975 C4 9-cylinder, 4-cycle, radial petrol/gasoline 460hp engine
Crew:	5
Main armament:	76mm M1A1, M1A1C or M1A2 in mount M62 in turret
Additional weapons:	Two .30cal Browning MG M1919A4; .50cal Browning MG HB M2 AA mount; 2-inch Mortar M3 smoke bomb thrower
Armour thickness:	0.5in to 3.5in (12mm to 88.9mm)
Max. road speed:	21mph (33.79km/h)
Total built:	3,426

Chapter 22

M4(105) Sherman Tank
Bastogne Barracks

Location: Set your navigation device to Bastogne Barracks, Rue de La-Roche 40, 6600 Bastogne, Belgium.

After World War Two, this M4(105) Sherman tank served in a Belgian Army fire-support platoon. A platoon was comprised of six M4(105) Sherman tanks. After decommissioning, the late L T G Dewandre, the founder of the Belgian Tank Museum, arranged for the tank to be put on display at the Royal Museum of Armed Forces and Military History in Brussels. During the 1980s, the tank was restored by former servicemen/volunteers. One was a veteran of the Belgian Army 3rd Lancers and painted the name 'Effronté' on the turret. The tank was moved to Bastogne Barracks for a full overhaul and is exhibited with the Belgium War Heritage Institute's collection of World War Two tanks. It has serial number 57304 and was built in June 1944.

The M4(105) Sherman Tank was armed with a 105mm M4 howitzer on an M52 mount. They did see service in the Ardennes. The US Army normally deployed M4(105) Shermans in a six-tank assault gun platoon. The howitzer was designed to be operated from a static position, like an artillery piece. They were not designed to take on enemy tanks at close quarters, but they did carry a couple of high explosive anti-tank (HEAT) rounds for self-defence if they were surprised. These tanks were used to provide close support to infantry and tank units when attacking concrete pillboxes, fortified farmhouses, soft-skinned lightly armoured vehicles, infantry concentrations and artillery batteries. It could fire a more powerful high explosive shell than Sherman tanks armed with a 75mm gun. The loader inserted the correct amount of charge (explosive propellant) needed to fire the high explosive round at the target into the base of the shell and then screwed on the base cap that contained the percussion primer M1B1A2. Longer range targets required more propellant.

Unlike open-topped M7 priest self-propelled artillery guns, the M4(105) Sherman gunner, loader and commander worked in a fully armoured enclosed turret. This meant the vehicle could work in an urban environment and get close to fortified strongpoints without fear of grenades being thrown into the fighting compartment and snipers firing from the upper levels of buildings.

M4(105) Shermans were not issued with wet ammunition stowage racks. They received armoured ammunition racks that could carry 66 105mm HE shells. Between February 1944 and March 1945, 1,641 M4(105) Shermans were produced. Under the Lend-Lease scheme, 593 entered service with British and Commonwealth forces.

Specifications	
Dimensions:	L: 20ft 4in (5.89m); W: 8ft 9in (2.61m); H: 9ft 7in (2.74m); Wt: 30.98 tons (31.47 tonnes)
Engine:	Continental R975 C1 9-cylinder, 4-cycle, radial petrol/gasoline 400hp engine
Crew:	5
Main armament:	105mm howitzer M4 in mount M52 in turret
Additional weapons:	Two .30cal Browning MG M1919A4; .50cal Browning MG HB M2 AA mount; 2in Mortar M3 smoke bomb thrower
Armour thickness:	0.5in to 3.6in (12mm to 91.44mm)
Max. road speed:	21mph (33.79km/h)
Total built:	75

Chapter 23

M32B1 Sherman Tank Recovery Vehicle
Bastogne Barracks

Location: Set your navigation device to Bastogne Barracks, Rue de La-Roche 40, 6600 Bastogne, Belgium.

This M32B1 Tank Recovery Vehicle is on display at the Bastogne Barracks. During the Battle of the Bulge, many damaged German tanks had to be abandoned on the battlefield due to the lack of recovery vehicles and repair facilities. A good example of this occurred on 24 December 1944, when five German 2nd SS Das Reich Panther tanks were damaged during an advance through a minefield between Manhay and Grandmenil. Although most only had track and suspension damage, their crews had to ignite internal explosive charges and leave them in the minefield. There were not enough Bergepanzer recovery tanks available. This was not the case with the US Army.

The M32B1 armoured recovery tank was based on the hull of an M4A1 Sherman tank built at the Lima Locomotive Works. This hull has the serial number 224. It was converted into a recovery tank by the Pressed Steel Car company in April 1943. It was equipped with a 60,000lb (26 ton) Gar Wood winch driven by a power take off from the tank's propeller shaft. Two boom arms were hinged to the front of the hull and supported by an 'A' shaped frame welded to the rear hull plate. Later versions had an additional 'A' frame fitted at the rear with a towing hook at the apex. They could be erected in the forward position when the winch was needed to act as a crane and lift an object like an engine. The M32B1 mechanical boom was raised by attaching a device to the right front sprocket. A cable was attached to it and the top of the 'A' frame. By driving the M32B1 forward, it lifted the 'A' Frame into position.

The boom arms were kept in the folded position to the rear when a tank or disabled vehicle needed to be towed. The winch was mounted inside the tank behind the driver's position, but the cable came out of an opening in the front armour in a central position. After World War Two, the Belgian Army used Sherman tank-based recovery vehicles. This M32B1 is fitted with WE210 'Rubber Standard' tracks originally fitted on an M3 Medium Grant tank. The original Sherman tank tracks were exchanged to enable a road worthy Sherman tank from the collection to be used on moving displays and events.

Specifications	
Dimensions:	L: without boom19ft 2in (5.84m), with 18ft (5.5m); W: 8ft 7in (2.61m); H: 9ft (2.74m); Wt: 28 tons (28.4 tonnes)
Engine:	Continental R975 C1 9-cylinder, 4-cycle, radial petrol/gasoline 400hp engine
Crew:	5
Main armament:	.30cal Browning MG M1919A4; .50cal Browning MG HB M2 AA mount; 81mm Mortar
Armour thickness:	0.5in to 2.0in (12mm to 50.8mm)
Max. road speed:	21mph (33.79km/h)
Total built:	1,055

Chapter 24

M5A1 Stuart Tank
Bastogne Barracks

Location: Set your navigation device to Bastogne Barracks, Rue de La-Roche 40, 6600 Bastogne, Belgium.

Stuart light tanks were used as scout tanks for reconnaissance work. Its gun was adequate for confronting lightly armoured enemy vehicles but could not penetrate the frontal armour of a Panzer IV, Panther or Tiger tank. It used its speed to get out of trouble and avoid becoming a target but was not always successful. Their smaller size compared to the Sherman and the slightly quieter engine was an advantage. Reconnaissance units would be sent ahead to see if bridges were still intact and to prevent them from being blown up by attacking the enemy engineers and infantry by the bridge. They would advance until they made contact with more heavily armed and armoured German forces and then radio back for help and call in an airstrike or an artillery barrage. They also provide support for defending infantry units.

Stuart tanks used in Normandy were sometimes fitted with a set of blades at the front. They were used to force an entry point through the high hedgerows that surrounded each field in the Normandy bocage country. Initially, these devices were fabricated in France, but later they were built in Britain and shipped to France. The construction of the first tank hedge cutter is credited to Sergeant Curtis G Culin, 102nd Cavalry Reconnaissance Squadron, 2nd Armored Division, based on a suggestion by a fellow soldier only known as 'Roberts'. They had different names: the 'Culin hedgerow cutter' or the 'Culin Rhino device'. Tanks fitted with the blades were sometimes given the nickname 'Rhino tanks' as they had 'tusks.'

This M5A1 Stuart has the markings of the US Army 9th Armored Division, 89th Cavalry Reconnaissance Squadron (Mechanized). They arrived in the Ardennes just prior to the beginning of the Battle of the Bulge.

After the war, the first ten tanks obtained by the Belgian Army were Stuarts. They were used to train new tank crews, who went on to operate Sherman 76mm and 17pdr gun tanks during the early years of the Cold War. The light tank reconnaissance role was soon taken over by M24 Chaffee and M41 Walter Bulldog light tanks. This is one of those Belgian Army Stuarts. It has been restored to a running condition.

Specifications	
Dimensions:	L: 15ft 10in (4.83m); W: 7ft 6in (2.28m); H: 8ft 5in (2.56m); Wt: 14.95 tons (15.19 tonnes)
Engine:	Twin Cadillac Series 42, 16-cylinder (eight per engine), 4-cycle, 296hp petrol/gasoline engine
Crew:	4
Main armament:	37mm gun M6 in mount M44 in the turret
Additional weapons:	.30cal Browning MG M1919A5 coaxial; .30cal Browning MG M1919A4 bow mount; .30cal Browning MG HB M2 AA mount
Armour thickness:	0.5in to 1.75in (12mm to 44.45mm)
Max. road speed:	36mph (57.93km/h)
Total built:	6,810

Chapter 25

M22 Locust Tank
Bastogne Barracks

Location: Set your navigation device to Bastogne Barracks, Rue de La-Roche 40, 6600 Bastogne, Belgium.

In 1941, the British expressed an interest in purchasing from America a very light tank that could be air portable and give support to lightly armed paratroops and glider-borne forces. The development contract was awarded to the Marmon-Harrington Company, Inc. They were already manufacturing light tanks for the United States Marine Corps, so they were seen as the perfect candidate to produce the United States' first air-mobile tank.

The prototype was too heavy and features like the bow machine guns and the power traverse had to be removed from the design. In April 1943, production of the Light Tank, M22 Locust, began at the Marmon-Harrington factory. A total of 820 tanks were constructed. The tank never saw combat with the US Army during World War Two. Under the Lend-Lease programme, 260 M22 Locust tanks were allocated to the British Army. Although the thickness of the front glacis plate armour was only 0.5in (12.7mm), it was equivalent to 1in (25.4mm) of vertical rolled homogeneous steel because of the high angle of slope. This also kept the weight of the tank down and was adequate to protect the crew from small-arms fire, high explosive and mortar shell shrapnel.

The M22 Locust could be carried by the British Hamilcar Mk.I glider in a battle-ready condition. The British version of the tank was fitted with smoke grenade launchers. Some had the 'Littlejohn' device fitted to the 37mm gun. This increased the velocity of the armour-piercing shells to increase their penetration power. The tank suffered from mechanical reliability problems.

On 24 March 1945, M22 Locust tanks did see action with the British during Operation *Varsity*, the airborne assault on the eastern bank of the Rhine River near the village of Hamminkeln and the town of Wesel. Their task was to secure that section of the river, enabling a successful surface river assault. Six tanks arrived in working order. Some had damage. One was knocked out. The others provided support for the American and British Airborne troops in the area.

Post-war, the Belgian Army used one M22 Locust as a tank driver training vehicle.

Specifications	
Dimensions:	L: 12ft 11in (3.96m); W: 7ft 1in (2.24m); H: 6ft 1in (1.84m); Wt: 74.3 tonnes (7.4 tons)
Engine:	Lycoming O-435T horizontally opposed 6-cylinder, 4-cycle, petrol/gasoline 192hp engine
Crew:	3
Main armament:	37mm Gun M6 in mount; M53 in turret
Additional weapons:	.30cal MG M1919A4
Armour thickness:	0.375in to 1.0in (9.5mm to 25.4mm)
Max. road speed:	35mph (56.3km/h)
Total built:	830

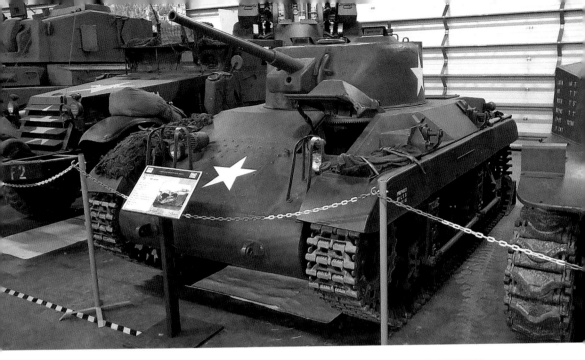

Chapter 26
M24 Chaffee Tank
Bastogne Barracks

Location: Set your navigation device to Bastogne Barracks, Rue de La-Roche 40, 6600 Bastogne, Belgium.

The M24 Chaffee, was intended as the replacement for the failed M7 light/medium tank design. It replaced M3/M5 Stuart light tanks. It was a leap forward in light tank design and had modern torsion bar suspensions, completely revised welded steel armour, improved protection and, more importantly, a much more powerful lightweight 75mm main gun. Although arriving late in the war, the Chaffee tank was a success. It was found to be efficient, simple, reliable and rugged. After the war, the tank was widely exported and stayed in service with many armies until the 1980s and beyond, encompassing most of the Cold War.

The US Army 740th Tank Battalion was rushed to the Ardennes but did not have time to be issued with tanks. They were authorized to collect whatever equipment they could find in local depots and went into combat armed with a jumble of vehicles that included two newly arrived M24 Chaffee light tanks, 90mm GMC M36 tank destroyers and British specification Sherman Tanks. This unit was the first to operate M24 Chaffee light tanks. More M24s were deployed to the battle as they became available. They continued to replace older Stuart light tanks until the end of the war.

At the end of World War Two, M24 Chaffee tanks saw service with the Belgian Army. They were used as light reconnaissance Cavalry tanks. M24s started to be decommissioned in 1958 and replaced by the M41 Walker Bulldog light tank. They were passed to reserve units. This M24 Chaffee saw service with the Belgian Army.

To keep the weight of the tank down, the armour was not very thick. The tank crews had to rely upon speed to get them out of trouble. The front glacis plate was 1in (25mm) thick. The top of the hull was only 0.40in (10mm) thick. The sides of the hull sloped inwards at the bottom. The thickness of the armour on the hull side of the M24 Chaffee was not uniform: the front two thirds of the armour were 1in (25mm) thick, but the last third of the side armour covering the engine compartment was only 0.75in (19mm) thick. The rear hull armour was 0.75in (19mm) thick. The turret armour was 1in (25mm) thick with the addition of a 1.5in (38mm)-thick gun mantlet.

Specifications	
Dimensions:	L: 18ft 2in (5.54m); W: 9ft 8in (2.98m); H: 9ft 1in (2.77m); Wt: 20.2 tons (18.32 tonnes)
Engine:	Twin Cadillac 44T24 8-cylinder, 4-cycle, petrol/gasoline 148hp engine
Crew:	5
Main armament:	75mm M6 gun in mount; M64 in turret
Additional weapons:	Two .30cal Browning MG M1919A4; .50cal Browning MG M2HB
Armour thickness:	0.4in to 1.5in (10mm to 38mm)
Max. road speed:	35mph (56km/h)
Total built:	4,731

Chapter 27
A12 Matilda II Tank
Bastogne Barracks

Location: Set your navigation device to Bastogne Barracks, Rue de La-Roche 40, 6600 Bastogne, Belgium.

In April 1934, the requirement for a heavily armoured tank mounting the new 2pdr anti-tank gun was issued. General Sir Hugh Elles had commanded the Tank Corps in World War One and was a firm believer in the need for tanks to support infantry during an assault. When he became Master General of the Ordnance in May 1934, he influenced the type of tank development that was undertaken by the Royal Arsenal, Woolwich, London. They produced the design of the Matilda II. The production order was awarded to the Vulcan Foundry to produce the first batch of 140 units by mid-1938.

Matilda II tanks did not see action during the Battle of the Bulge. This vehicle came from the Cadman Collection in the UK. The tank's engine had been removed. The Matilda II, Infantry tank Mk.II, A12 was one of the few tanks that saw service throughout the entire length of World War Two. During the fighting in France and Belgium in 1940, the British Matilda II tank's 2pdr gun could knock out advancing Panzer II, Panzer 38(t), Panzer III and Panzer IV German tanks. The German 3.7mm anti-tank gun could not penetrate the Matilda's thick 78mm armour. The French Char B1 bis heavy tank only had 60mm of armour. In early 1940, the German Panzer III and IV tanks had 30mm thick frontal armour. In the early North African desert campaigns, the 2pdr armour-piercing shell could penetrate the armour of every Italian tank. By 1942, the 2pdr was considered obsolete as enemy tank designs had up-armoured.

The Matilda II was designed as an 'infantry tank' rather than a fast 'cruiser tank.' It was intended to work closely with the infantry, providing a heavily armoured anti-tank resource, and therefore speed was not a major requirement. The tank continued to be used in the Far East until the end of the war, as Japanese tanks did not have thick armour. Matilda II tanks were not issued with high explosive shells, but its thick amour enabled it to get safely close to enemy machine gun nests and neutralise them with its 7.92mm Besa machine gun.

Specifications	
Dimensions:	L: 18ft 5in (5.61m); W: 8ft 6in (2.59m); H: 8ft 3in (2.51m); Wt: 25.5 tons (25.6 tonnes)
Engine:	Two AEC or two Leyland straight 6-cylinder, water-cooled, diesel 95hp engines
Crew:	4
Main armament:	QF 2pdr (40mm)
Additional weapons:	7.92mm Besa machine gun
Armour thickness:	0.8in to 3.1in (20mm to 78mm)
Max. road speed:	15mph (24.1km/h)
Total built:	2,987

Chapter 28

Panzerbefehlswagen IV Ausf. J Command Tank
Bastogne Barracks

Location: Set your navigation device to Bastogne Barracks, Rue de La-Roche 40, 6600 Bastogne, Belgium.

From March 1944, 88 Panzer IV Ausf. J tanks were converted to be Panzerbefehlswagen (Pz.Bef. Wg.) command tanks. Only an additional 17 were built as Panzerbefehlswagen at the factory. Additional long-range radio sets were installed along with mounting racks, transformers, junction boxes, wiring, antenna mounts and an extra generator to power this equipment. The extra space needed resulted in a loss of stowage room for ammunition. The amount of 75mm rounds was reduced to 72 shells, compared to 87 held in other platoon Panzer IV tanks. Most of the changes occurred inside the tank, but there are a couple of minor exterior differences between the Pz.Bef. Wg. IV Ausf. J and standard Panzer IV Ausf. J. The most notable of these was the addition of antennas for the new radio equipment. At the rear, there was a 'star' antenna (Sternantenne D) for the Fu 8 radio, a 6.6ft (2m) antenna for a Fu 5 radio and finally 4.6ft (1.4m) antenna for a Fu 7 radio.

German Panzer IV tanks took part in the Battle of the Bulge in December 1944, but this particular tank on display in the Bastogne Barracks did not. It has the Fahrgestell serial number 92200 and was constructed in September 1944 by the Nibelungenwerke factory, Austria. Following its capture in Belgium, it was shipped to the US Army Ordnance Museum in Aberdeen, Maryland, US. It was the subject of the European Theater of Operations ETO Report 172. As part of an exchange for some World War One artillery howitzers, it went to Germany and then to Belgium.

Starting from May 1943, Schürzen skirt armour was fitted to the side of the Panzer IV tanks and around the turret. It is missing from the hull on this tank, but the skirt armour 'L' shaped 'hangers' can still be seen jutting off the track guard on the side of the tank. They were fitted to protect the tank's hull. The side armour was thin and vulnerable to penetration from Soviet infantry operated 14.5mm anti-tank rifles. Soviet troops were instructed to shoot these weapons at the enemy tank's side armour. The lower hull side armour thickness and the sides and rear armour on the turret were only 30mm thick.

Specifications	
Dimensions:	L: 23ft (7.02m); W: 9ft 5in (2.88m); H: 8ft 9.5in (2.68m); Wt: 24.6 tons (25 tonnes)
Engine:	Maybach HL 120 TRM V12, 265hp petrol/gasoline engine
Crew:	5
Main armament:	7.5cm Kw.K.40 L/48
Additional weapons:	Two 7.92mm M.G.34 machine guns
Armour thickness:	0.3in to 3in (8mm to 80mm)
Max. road speed:	23.6mph (38km/h)
Total converted/built:	88/17

Chapter 29

Sturmgeschütz 40 Ausf. F/8 Assault Gun (Sd.Kfz.142)
Bastogne Barracks

Location: Set your navigation device to Bastogne Barracks, Rue de La-Roche 40, 6600 Bastogne, Belgium.

This Sturmgeschütz 40 Ausführung F/8 assault gun is rare, as it is only one of three known surviving examples. It was captured by US troops in Sicily prior to the assault on the Italian mainland. This vehicle was then shipped to the Aberdeen Proving Ground in Maryland, US, for testing. In the 1960s, it was given to Germany and displayed for several years in the instructional collection of the Panzertruppenschule (amour training school) in Munster. It was then transferred to the German Scientific Collection of Defence Engineering Specimens (WTS) at Koblenz. In the early 1980s, following an exchange for some World War One artillery pieces and a few other vehicles, it was transported to and put on display at the Royal Museum of the Armed Forces and Military History in Brussels. Following the decision to house the Belgium War Heritage Institute's World War Two vehicle collection in Bastogne Barracks, it was moved to its final resting place.

The German Sturmgeschütz assault gun (StuG III) was based on a Panzer III tank hull. It was originally designed as a fully armoured, direct fire artillery weapon intended to support the infantry. On 28 September 1941, following the receipt of combat reports on the problems encountered by German troops having to defend themselves against attacks by the new Soviet T-34 and KV-1 tanks, German High Command (OKH) sent a request to Hitler. It asked for the armour on the StuG III to be increased and a high-velocity 7.5cm long barrel anti-tank gun to be fitted so they could deal with this new threat.

The new version of the StuG was armed with the 7.5cm Stu.K.40 L/48 gun. The front of the superstructure had to be redesigned to take the larger recoil and recuperator cylinders. The new box mantlet armour was 2in (50mm) thick. The front armour was also 50mm thick, but 1.2in (30mm) thick additional armour plates were added to make the front armour 3in (80mm) thick. The first Sturmgeschütz 40 Ausf. F/8 was constructed in late October/early November 1942 by Alkett and then stopped in December 1942. Some that were shipped to North Africa and Southern Europe were painted in the tropen camouflage scheme two-thirds gelbbraun (yellow-brown) and one-third graugrün (grey-green). The remainder were painted dunkelgrau (dark grey). On 18 February 1943, Inspectorate 2 issued an order to paint all new armoured vehicles in a base coat of dunkelgelb (dark yellow).

Specifications	
Dimensions:	L: 20ft 8in (6.31m); W: 9ft 8in (2.95m); H: 7ft ½in (2.15m); Wt: 25.57 tons (23.2 tonnes)
Engine:	Maybach HL 120 TRM V12, water-cooled, 11.9 litre, 265hp petrol/gasoline engine
Crew:	4
Main armament:	7.5cm Stu.K. L/48 gun
Additional weapons:	7.92mm M.G.34 machine gun
Armour thickness:	0.39in to 3.14in (10mm to 80mm)
Max. road speed:	25mph (40km/h)
Total built:	250

Chapter 30

Loyd Carrier and Renault UE
Bastogne Barracks

Location: Set your navigation device to Bastogne Barracks, Rue de La-Roche 40, 6600 Bastogne, Belgium.

In World War One, the British converted some tanks to be armoured supply vehicles that could follow the attacking tanks across the battlefield and be in a position to resupply them with ammunition and fuel. This saved the tanks from having to drive all the way back to the British start line. The French also converted some of their Schneider tanks to fulfil the same role. Between the wars, the French and the British experimented in designing armoured supply vehicles and tractors that could tow artillery guns and keep the crew safe from small-arms fire.

The Renault UE was the most produced tracked armoured vehicle in the French Army before World War Two. Its main job was to transport supplies to infantry units on the front line. Items could be stacked in the armoured tracked trailer or in the rear stowage compartment on the back of the vehicle. The driver's and commander's heads were protected by individual domed cupolas that had vision slits in them. Outside of the combat area, they could be flipped backwards to give the crew better vision. The letters UE are not an abbreviation, they are just the Renault factory code for this vehicle construction project.

Many Renault UE vehicles were captured in France by the occupying German army and entered into service. The original Renault UE was not armed. The Germans altered some of their vehicles to enable an armoured cabin to be fitted so that a machine gun could be mounted. These vehicles would perform security and policing roles.

The British Loyd Carrier upper hull was enclosed with armour plate at the sides and front but open at the rear. It did not have an armoured roof. It was not intended to be a frontline fighting vehicle. A 2-inch mortar and single Bren light machine gun were sometimes carried for self-defence purposes. It was a multi-role vehicle. The Tracked Personnel Carrier (TPC) variant could transport eight soldiers or the equivalent weight in cargo. The Tracked Towing (TT) version was used to tow either the ML 4.2-inch mortar, QF 2pdr or 6pdr anti-tank guns and their crews.

Specifications	Loyd Carrier	Renault UE
Dimensions:	L: 13ft 11in (4.24m); W: 6ft 9in (2.06m); H: 4ft 8in (1.42m); Wt: 4.50 tons (4.57 tonnes)	L: 9ft 2in (2.8m); W: 5ft 9in (1.74m); H: 4ft 1in (1.25m); Wt: 2.63 tonnes (2.58 tons)
Engine:	Ford V8 side valve petrol/gasoline 85hp engine	Renault 85 4-cylinder 38hp engine
Vehicle crew:	1	2
Towed weapons:	Towed 2pdr or 6pdr anti-tank guns; towed ML 4.2-inch mortar	None
Self-defence weapons:	Bren gun and 2-inch mortar stowed against the engine cover	None
Armour thickness:	Up to 7mm (0.27in)	Up to 0.35in (9mm)
Max. road speed:	30mph (48km/h)	19mph (30km/h)
Total built:	Over 16,000	5, 168 in France, 126 in Romania

Chapter 31

Sexton 25pdr Mk.II SP
Bastogne Barracks

Location: Set your navigation device to Bastogne Barracks, Rue de La-Roche 40, 6600 Bastogne, Belgium.

Sexton 25pdr Artillery self-propelled guns were used by the British during the Battle of the Bulge. The first Sextons were based on the American M3 Lee tank hull, but then the Canadian-built M4 Sherman Grizzley tank hull was chosen to replace it. The Sexton was powered by a Continental R-975 9-cylinder radial petrol engine that produced 400hp. It had a top speed of 24mph (38.6km/h), which meant that it could keep up with British and Commonwealth armour during an attack. They were not meant to be at the front of an attack. They would fire their high explosive shells over the heads of the infantry and tanks in the front line onto enemy positions. The crews would rarely see their target. They would be sent 'fire missions' as a grid reference by radio and plot them on a map. This form of attack was called 'indirect fire'.

They needed to keep up with the attacking troops so they could continue to give them artillery support as they pressed forward. A self-propelled gun battery was quicker to set up than a battery of towed field howitzers. They could also redeploy to another location faster. Most batteries had a forward observation officer who would go forward to the front line and radio back grid references and give corrections if the shells were falling too short or too long. Infantry and armoured reconnaissance teams could also radio for an artillery barrage to deal with concentrations of enemy troops.

The Sexton had a crew of six: commander, driver, gunner, gun-layer, loader and radio operator. They were protected from small-arms fire, high explosive and mortar shell shrapnel by an open-top armoured superstructure that ranged in thickness from 15mm to 32mm. The hull armour ranged from 12.7mm to 50.8mm.

Sextons were armed with the QF 25pdr howitzer (87.6mm) Mk.II and carried 105 rounds of mainly high explosive shells. Some were smoke rounds, and a few were armour-piercing rounds in case of a surprise attack by a German tank. For self-defence, Sexton crews were issued with 0.303cal Bren light machine guns, 0.303cal rifles and 9mm Sten submachine guns. This Sexton is waiting its turn to be restored.

Specifications	
Dimensions:	L: 20ft 1in (6.12m); W: 8ft 11in (2.71m); H: 8ft (2.43m); Wt: 25.44 tons (25.8 tonnes)
Engine:	Continental R975 C4 9-cylinder, 4-cycle, radial petrol/gasoline 400hp
Crew:	6
Main armament:	QF 25pdr howitzer (87.6mm) Mk. II
Additional weapons:	Two .303cal Bren machine guns; two .303cal Rifles No 4; two 9mm Sten submachine guns
Armour thickness:	0.5in to 2.0in (12.7mm to 50.8mm)
Max. road speed:	24mph (38.6km/h)
Total built:	Around 2,000

Chapter 32

Valentine Mk.IX Tank
Bastogne Barracks

Location: Set your navigation device to Bastogne Barracks, Rue de La-Roche 40, 6600 Bastogne, Belgium.

This Valentine IX came from the Military Museum in Delft, the Netherlands. It is missing the muzzle brake and stowage boxes on the right-side track guard. Valentine gun tanks were not used during the Battle of the Bulge; in fact, by late 1944, they were considered obsolete. Its official designation was Tank, Infantry, Mark III, Valentine IX. The Belgian Army did not use them post-World War Two.

Before the start of World War Two, British military doctrine required that the army had four different types of tanks to fulfil specific roles: light tanks were used for reconnaissance tasks; well-armed and fast 'cuiser' tanks took on the role of the cavalry: slow and heavily armoured 'infantry' tanks were meant to support advancing infantry; heavy assault tanks were designed to overcome enemy defensive structures. The Valentine was designed to be an infantry tank, along with the Matilda II and the later Churchill tanks.

To keep the development time short, the engineers used the same engine, transmission, drivetrain, suspension, road wheels and tracks fitted to the A9 and A10 cruiser tanks. What made it an infantry tank rather than a cruiser tank was its thick armour. This additional weight reduced its maximum speed.

In 1942, the Valentine tank's 2pdr gun was found to be inadequate. Most of the German Panzer III or IV tanks, after the battle for France in May 1940, had their frontal armour thickness increased to 50mm or 60mm. Vickers engineers adapted the more powerful long-barrel QF 6pdr (57mm/2.24in) anti-tank gun so that it could be mounted into the cramped Mark III turret. They succeeded, but the coaxial .30cal Besa machine gun had to be removed.

Official British War Department test figures show that the 6pdr Mk.V anti-tank gun firing armour-piercing (AP) rounds would penetrate the following thickness of homogeneous armour plate at these distances: 500 yards (457m) = 85.5mm; 1,000 yards (914.4m) = 72.5mm and 1,500 yards (1371.6m) = 60.4mm. When firing armour-piercing capped (APC) rounds at face-hardened armour plate these are the test results: 500 yards (457m) = 93.8mm; 1,000 yards (914.4m) = 76.3mm and 1,500 yards (1371.6m) = 61.25m. In 1942–43, the Valentine IX tank could knock out most German tanks. It could not penetrate the frontal armour of the Tiger and Panther tank, but its shells could penetrate those tank's side and rear armour.

Specifications	
Dimensions:	L: 19ft 5in (5.92m); W: 8ft 5in (2.57m); H: 6ft 11.5in (2.12m); Wt: 17.20 tons (17.45 tonnes)
Engine:	GMC 6004 diesel 165hp engine
Crew:	3
Main armament:	QF 6pdr (57mm) Mk.III or Mk.V with counter weights on muzzle
Additional weapons:	No machine guns; two 4in smoke round projectors on right side
Armour thickness:	0.78in to 2.56in (20mm to 65mm)
Max. road speed:	15mph (24km/h)
Total built:	1,087 (+236 Duplex Drive swimming tanks)

Chapter 33
A34 Comet Tank
Bastogne Barracks

Location: Set your navigation device to Bastogne Barracks, Rue de La-Roche 40, 6600 Bastogne, Belgium.

This World War Two British-built tank saw service with the Irish Army during the Cold War. After it was decommissioned, the tank was put on display in the Royal Museum of the Armed Forces and Military History in Brussels. It was then temporarily stored at the Kapellen military base before being moved to Bastogne Barracks.

The highly successful British A41 Centurion tank was under development during the last years of World War Two, but it would not be ready in time to see combat. The British needed a stop-gap tank. The 17pdr anti-tank gun had proved effective in stopping German tanks in North Africa. Work was started to fit a 17pdr gun into an up-armoured turret mounted on a late version Cromwell tank hull. It was given the designation A34, Cruiser Tank, Comet Mark I type A. The Cromwell tank was fast and had a low profile. Using a pre-existing tank hull design cut down the development time. A larger turret ring was required to cope with the bigger turret needed for the Comet tank. By December 1944, only 31 Comet tanks had arrived in northwest Europe, and they were not used during the Battle of the Bulge. Although 3,000 had been ordered, only 1,186 were built. The end of the war resulted in an early cancellation of the full order. These vehicles saw combat in the Netherlands and Germany, but they started to be replaced by Centurion tanks in 1949. A few continued in British Army service in Berlin until 1957 and Hong Kong until 1959.

The new 3in (76.2mm) high-velocity tank gun that was fitted to the Comet was called the QF 77mm HV gun. This designation was used to avoid confusion with the Sherman Firefly 76.2mm 17pdr gun and the American Sherman 76.2mm tank gun. Vickers-Armstrongs redesigned the Comet gun's breech and recoil system to fit inside the new turret. The shell cartridge and charge size were reduced. This decreased the hitting power by around 10 per cent, but it was found to be more accurate at longer distances than the Sherman Firefly's 17pdr gun.

Specifications	
Dimensions:	L: 21ft 6in (6.55m); W: 10ft 1in (3.04m); H: 8ft 6in (2.67m); Wt: 32.7 tons (33.53 tonnes)
Engine:	Rolls Royce Meteor Mk.III, V12 petrol/gasoline 600hp engine
Crew:	5
Main armament:	QF 77mm HV gun
Additional weapons:	Two 7.92mm Besa machine guns
Armour thickness:	1.26in to 4.02in (32mm to 102mm)
Max. road speed:	32mph (51km/h)
Total built:	1,186

Chapter 34

Soviet ISU-152M, T-34-85 and IS-3M Tank

Bastogne Barracks

Location: Set your navigation device to Bastogne Barracks, Rue de La-Roche 40, 6600 Bastogne, Belgium.

In 1988, staff at the Belgian Tank Museum were restoring the exterior of a Czechoslovakian-built Soviet T-34-85 that had been donated by the West German government. They asked Colonel Orloff, the Soviet military attaché to Belgium, what paint type and markings should be used. He suggested painting the tank in 'the earth colour found in Ukraine after the harvest and applying the markings of the Soviet Great Armour Regiment.' They also asked how to request an IS-3 and ISU-152 SPG for the museum's collection. They followed his instructions and submitted a letter to the Soviet Ministry of Defence via the Russian ambassador in Belgium. In September 1988, a goodwill gift of the two requested Soviet vehicles arrived, along with spare parts for the T-34-85, Soviet tank crew uniforms and three instructors for a week who would teach the museum staff how to drive and maintain the vehicles. Both had come from the reserve collection of the Kiev Military Museum. On 7 September 1945, the unexpected public appearance of the IS-3 tank during the post-war Allied Victory Parade in Berlin caused a great deal of concern in the West. Its thick, sloped 'pike-nosed' hull armour, low profile curved turret, and powerful 122mm D-25T gun made it a formidable threat. They had been rushed to Germany in the final months of war but did not see combat.

The ISU-152 self-propelled gun had three roles: assault gun, tank destroyer and mobile artillery. Its thickly armoured, fully enclosed superstructure meant that it could be used in an urban environment. The 152.4mm ML-20S howitzer's heavy shells could 'overmatch' the armour of every German tank. All three vehicles were built post-war. They were fitted with wide tracks to reduce the overall ground pressure exerted by the vehicle and help them cross rough, muddy ground. The letter 'M' indicates they received upgrades as part of the modernisation scheme.

Specifications	ISU-152M	T-34-85	IS-3M
Dimensions:	L: 30ft 1in (9.18m); W: 10ft 1in (3.07m); H: 8ft 1in (2.48m); Wt: 46.5 tons (47.3 tonnes)	L: 26ft 9in (8.15m); W: 9ft 10in (3m); H: 8ft 6in (2.6m); Wt: 31.5 tons (32 tonnes)	L: 32ft 4in (9.85m); W: 10ft 1.65in (3.09m); H: 8ft (2.45m); Wt: 53.8 tons (54.7 tonnes)
Engine:	V-2IS 12-cylinder, 4-stroke diesel 520hp	V2 38.8L diesel 500hp	V-2-1S V12 diesel 600hp
Main armament:	152.4mm ML-20S howitzer	85mm ZiS-S-53, 85mm S-53 or 85mm D-5T	122mm D-25T gun
Additional weapons:	12.7mm DhSK anti-aircraft machine gun	Two 7.62mm DT machine guns	Two 7.62mm DT machine guns; 12.7mm (0.5in) DShK anti-aircraft machine gun
Armour thickness:	3.54in to 4.72in (90mm to 120mm)	1.18in to 3.54in (30mm to 90mm)	2.36in to 6.89in (60mm to 175mm)
Max. road speed:	18.6mph (30km/h)	23.6mph (38km/h)	25mph (40km/h)

Chapter 35
M47 Patton Tank
Bastogne Barracks

Location: Set your navigation device to Bastogne Barracks, Rue de La-Roche 40, 6600 Bastogne, Belgium.

During the Cold War, the Belgian Army received 773 US-built M47 Patton tanks to equip its tank regiments stationed in Germany. It was a complicated machine compared to the World War Two-era tanks it replaced. The two bulges on the side of the turret are the protective armoured housing for the M12 stereoscopic range finder. It took a lot of training to master, but when the gunner was proficient, the 90mm M36 was a very effective and accurate weapon. When used correctly, it could improve first-hit probability. The Continental AV-1790-5B V12, air-cooled, twin-turbo petrol/gasoline 810hp engine was a lot quieter compared to the noisy Leopard I engine, but the large hot exhaust deflectors at the rear meant that it could easily be spotted by enemy gunners using infrared target acquisition equipment. The M47 Patton was the last US medium tank to be armed with a bow machine gun.

It only saw a few years of service in the US Army and was replaced in 1953 by the M48 Patton tank. The tank was rushed into production as the Korean War had started. To keep things simple, the M46 Patton tank's hull, engine, transmission, and drivetrain were kept with few modifications. The main change was the fitting of a larger turret to house the 90mm gun. Production started in May 1952 at the Detroit Tank Arsenal and later at the American Locomotive Company. The M47 Patton tank was successfully exported to several countries around the world. The M47 tank was sometimes called the 'Patton II' to differentiate it from the M46 Patton tank.

When West Germany joined NATO in May 1955, the Belgian Army in Germany changed from being one of occupation to an 'army of protection.' In the event of a Warsaw Pact attack, they were allocated a 60km (37 miles) wide sector to defend. It ran from the Belgium border with West Germany to the East German border and was known as the FBA-BSD sector. At the height of the Cold War, 40,000 Belgian soldiers were stationed in Germany. Many were conscripts completing their National Service. The last remaining Belgium soldiers stationed in Germany left in 2005.

Specifications	
Dimensions:	L: 27ft 11in (8.51m); W: 11ft 6in (3.51m); H: 10ft 1in (3.32m); Wt: 45.45 tons (46.17 tonnes)
Engine:	Continental AV-1790-5B 12-cylinder, 4-cycle petrol/gasoline 810hp (or AV-1790-7, AV-1790-7B)
Crew:	5
Main armament:	90mm M36 (T119E1) in M78 mount in turret
Additional weapons:	Two .30cal Browning M1919A4E1 machine guns; .50cal Browning M2 machine gun
Armour thickness:	0.5in to 4.5in (13mm to 144mm)
Max. road speed:	30mph (48km/h)
Total built:	8,576 (Detroit Arsenal 5,481; ALC 3,095)

Chapter 36

A27M Cromwell Tank
Bastogne Barracks

Location: Set your navigation device to Bastogne Barracks, Rue de La-Roche 40, 6600 Bastogne, Belgium.

The Cromwell tank was more agile than Sherman and Churchill tanks used by other British and Commonwealth armoured units. The tank first saw action following the landings in Normandy on D-Day. Its designation was Cruiser Tank Mark VIII A27M Cromwell. The letter 'M' signifies the tank was fitted with a Meteor engine. (The A27L Centaur was fitted with a Nuffield Liberty engine.) It was armed with a QF 75mm gun that had been adapted from the QF 6pdr gun to enable it to fire the US M3 75mm ammunition used in the Sherman tank while using the same 6pdr gun mount. The 75mm high explosive shell was effective in infantry support situations. The AP rounds could penetrate the side and rear armour of most German tanks but not the frontal armour of the Panther and Tiger tanks. To counteract this problem, a troop of three Cromwell tanks normally operated with a fourth tank armed with the high-velocity 17pdr gun in an 'overwatch' role. Initially, this role was given to a Sherman Firefly, but they were later replaced by an A30 Challenger tank when they became available.

On 3 September 1944, Brussels was liberated. The Guards Armoured Division, after a high-speed run, advancing 75 miles in one day, entered through the east of the city. The first tanks to drive into Place Poelaert and be photographed in front of the Palais de Justice and World War One monuments to the fallen were Cromwell tanks. The Belgian Tank Museum purchased a Cromwell to represent these tanks. It was a Cold War British Army FV4101 Charioteer tank that had been sold to the Finnish Army. When they no longer needed them, they were sold and exported back to Britain. It was then converted back to the specifications of a World War Two Cromwell tank. The conversion work for the historical TV series *Band of Brothers* was done by R&R Motor Services in Kent. The tank was sold after filming and put up for auction some years later. It went to Bastogne via the workshops of the Norfolk Tank Museum. Adrian Barrel assisted in making replica parts, such as stowage bins. The smaller Cromwell turret was modified to fit on the larger Charioteer turret ring. It only had a dummy gun for the film work. A Cromwell gun barrel and muzzle brake were found and fitted. It does not have a gun breech or recoil mechanism.

Specifications	
Dimensions:	L: 21ft 10in (6.65m); W: 9ft 6in (2.89m); H: 7ft 9in (2.36m); Wt: 27 tons (27.43 tonnes)
Engine:	Rolls-Royce Meteor, V12 600hp engine
Crew:	5
Main armament:	QF 75mm
Additional weapons:	Two 7.92mm Besa machine guns
Armour thickness:	0.25in to 2.5in (6.35mm to 63.5mm)
Max. road speed:	39.2mph (63km/h)
Total built:	2368 riveted, 126 welded

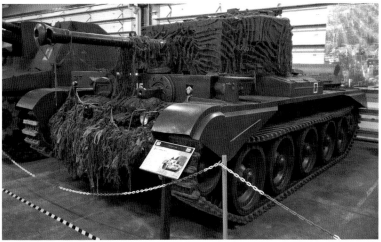

Chapter 37
M4A3 Sherman Tank Barracuda
Bastogne Town Centre

Location: Set your navigation device to Place Général McAuliffe, 6600 Bastogne, Belgium.

On 30 December 1944, this M4A3 Sherman tank named 'Barracuda' was knocked out between the villages of Renuâmont and Hubermont. It has the serial number S48935 USA 3081532 and was built at Fisher. It served with Company B, 41st Tank Battalion, 11th Armored Division. On 30 December 1944, two Shermans drove past the electric hut at the Hubermont crossroads and headed northeast across the snow-covered, muddy field towards Renuâmont, which was on a hill in front of them. German forces still occupied the village and the surrounding woodland. Barracuda was spotted by the crew of a Panzer IV. The Shermans got stuck in the muddy ground near the stream that ran across the field. An armour-piercing round hit the left side of the Sherman and knocked the tank out. The tank was also hit by a panzerfaust in the rear. The crew were captured, including the tank commander Staff Sergeant Wallace R Alexander, who had been badly wounded in the leg. Unfortunately, he died of his wounds in a prisoner of war camp a few days later. The other four stayed in captivity until the end of the war and returned home safely. The other Sherman, commanded by Captain Ameno, was also knocked out. None of the crew survived.

After the war, like many of the other abandoned tanks in the Ardennes, this tank was intended to be sent to the scrap metal steel foundry in Liège. However, the farmer refused permission for the tank to be cut up in his field. He did not want engine oil, grease and fuel to pollute the stream and the meadow he used to graze his animals. The tank was not cut up but dragged out of the field and transported 10km to the centre of Bastogne. In 1946, it was put on display in the centre of the town as a tribute to the men of the US Army. A replacement turret was fitted.

Specifications	
Dimensions:	L: 19ft 4in (5.90m); W: 8ft 7in (2.61m); H: 9ft (2.74m); Wt: 29.77 tons (31.61 tonnes)
Engine:	Ford GAA 8-cylinder, 4-cycle, petrol/gasoline 500hp engine
Crew:	5
Main armament:	75mm M3 gun in mount M34A1 in turret
Additional weapons:	Two .30cal Browning MG M1919A4 .50cal. Browning MG HB M2 AA mount 2in Mortar M3 smoke bomb thrower
Armour thickness:	0.5in to 3.5in (12mm to 88.9mm)
Max. road speed:	26mph (41.8km/h)
Total built:	1,690

Chapter 38

M10 17pdr SP Achilles IIC
Arlon

Location: Set your navigation device to Place Léopold 1,6700 Arlon, Belgium. On 31 March 2021, the Achilles was transported to workshops to get a new coat of paint. On its return, the town council want to move it to a new location, Place Schalbert, Arlon, by the Patton monument. Before travelling, check with the tourist office that it has returned and where it has been placed.

In September 1984, the local tourist office wanted to dramatically commemorate the 40th anniversary of the liberation of Arlon on 10 September 1944 by US Army forces. Plans were made for a World War Two tank destroyer to be used as a permanent war memorial centrepiece in the town's marketplace as a sign of gratitude to the American troops for driving out the German invaders.

After the war, the Belgian Army was supplied with ex-Canadian Army M10 17pdr SP Achilles IIC self-propelled guns under the Major Defense Acquisition Programs (MDAP). They were issued to Belgian Army anti-tank battalions. At the end of their service life, they were decommissioned and put into storage. Some were used as hard targets on firing ranges, and others were kept as replacement targets. Several were transported to the Belgian Army Training ground at Camp Lagland, southwest of Arlon, to be used as instructional vehicles for new students.

The tank destroyer on display in Arlon was one of those Achilles. It has the serial number of 742 and was built by Fisher in October 1943. It does not have an original 17pdr gun barrel. It has been painted to look like a US Army 3-inch GMC M10 tank destroyer. The series of numbers and letters in white paint on the vehicle infer that it was the 5th unit of Company A, 630th Tank Destroyer Battalion, 3rd Army.

On 10 September 1944, the 630th Tank Destroyer Battalion unit report records that the 1st Reconnaissance Platoon attached to Company A entered Arlon at 1.16pm, followed by the whole company at 4pm. Arlon was liberated on that date from German occupation. On 11 September 1944, Company A placed its guns in positions around Arlon to provide night-time defence for US Army Task Force S, commanded by Lieutenant Colonel Daniel B Strickler.

The 630th Tank Destroyer Battalion was involved in heavy fighting when the Ardennes offensive started. They officially operated towed 3-inch anti-tank guns, but a unit report dated 2 January 1945 mentions the use of four 3-inch GMC M10 tank destroyers being held in mobile reserve. They converted to 90mm GMC M36 tank destroyers in April 1945.

Specifications	
Dimensions:	L: 23ft 10in (7.27m); W: 10ft (3.04m); H over AA gun: 9ft 6in (2.89m); Wt: 29.10 tons (29.57 tonnes)
Engine:	General Motors 6046, 12-cylinder, 2-cycle, twin in-line diesel 410hp engine
Crew:	5
Main armament:	QF 17pdr in turret mount; No.3 Mk.1 in turret
Additional weapons:	.50cal MG HB M2 AA mount on turret; 2-inch muzzle loading mortar
Armour thickness:	0.375in to 2.25in (9.5mm to 57mm)
Max. road speed:	30mph (48.2km/h)
Total built:	Achilles = 1,100, M10 = 4,993, M10A1 = 1,713

Chapter 39

M4A1 Sherman Tank
Ettelbruck

Location: Set your navigation device to Patton Monument, 102 Avenue J-F Kennedy, 9147 Erpeldange-sur-Sûre, Luxembourg. It is about 650m northwest of Ettelbruck on the N7, just before the bridge over the railway and the Sûre River.

O n 25 December 1944, troops of the US 3rd Army liberated the town of Ettlebruck. The M4A1 Sherman came from the French Army. It has the serial number 29178 and was manufactured by the Pressed Steel Car company in July 1943.

The tank has been painted to resemble a Sherman of the 5th Armored Division, 34th Tank Battalion, Company B, unit 12. This tank forms part of the General Patton Memorial at Ettelbruck. It used to be a Sherman Dozer but has been restored as a standard M4A1 tank with a 75mm gun.

The Sherman Dozer was a valuable battlefield tool. In 1943, a field modification added a hydraulic dozer blade from an industrial Caterpillar D8 to a Sherman Tank. The later M1 dozer blade was standardised to fit any Sherman with VVSS suspension, and the M1A1 version would fit the wider HVSS. Some M4s made for the engineering corps had blades fitted permanently and the turrets removed.

Dozer tanks were used on the D-Day beaches to construct sand and earth ramps over tank obstacles. They were also used to fill in anti-tank ditches. In the countryside, they would clear road obstructions and move knocked out tanks to the side of the road so others could pass. They were also used to break through hedgerows in the Normandy bocage country. When the dozer blade was not required, they were unbolted. If you look at the middle suspension bogie, you will see a square bracket with four holes in it. This was the Sherman dozer blade fixing point. Another clue to indicate this tank was fitted with a dozer blade can be seen by the side of the hull machine gun. There are the remains of a 'U' shaped pipe. This was the hydraulic hose attachment. Three additional pieces of appliqué armour have been welded to the side of the tank hull. The one on the left was to give extra protection to the driver. The one on the right at the front protected the hull machine gunner. The third piece of additional armour on the right side of the tanks was to give extra protection to the ammunition stowage bins.

Specifications	
Dimensions:	L: 19ft 2in (5.84m); W: 8ft 7in (2.61m); H: 9ft (2.74m); Wt: 29.82 tons (30.2 tonnes)
Engine:	Continental R975 C1 9-cylinder, 4-cycle, radial petrol/gasoline 400hp engine
Crew:	5
Main armament:	75mm M3 gun in mount M34 in turret
Additional weapons:	Two .30cal Browning MG M1919A4; .50cal Browning MG HB M2 AA mount
Armour thickness:	0.5in to 3.0in (12mm to 76.2mm)
Max. road speed:	21mph (33.79km/h)
Total built:	6,281

Chapter 40

M4A1(76)W Sherman Tank
Diekirch

Location: Set your navigation device to 10 Bamertal, 9209 Dikrech, Luxembourg. This is the Musée National d'Histoire Militaire Diekirch (National Museum of Military History). Be careful of the speed cameras.

This M4A1(76)W Sherman Tank had been in service with the Dutch Army during the Cold War. When it was replaced by more modern tanks, this Sherman was transported to the National Museum of Military History in Diekirch. On 24 August 2018, it was cosmetically restored again. The unit markings of the US Army, 37th Tank Battalion, 4th Armored Division were added to enable the Museum to tell the story of Captain James 'Jimmie' H Leach, former commanding officer of B Company, 37th Tank Battalion.

On 24 December 1944, Captain Leach led his company in an attack on the strongly defended town of Bigonville in Luxembourg, 35km west of Diekirch. The Germans managed to destroy two of his tanks. Captain Leach suffered a head injury. Despite this, he and his men continued their assault on Bigonville. Leach was wounded a second time, but he did not cease to lead the attack until the enemy was defeated and the town of Bigonville secured. For his leadership during the liberation of Bigonville, Captain Jimmie Leach was awarded the Distinguished Service Cross for extraordinary heroism during the Battle of the Bulge. He was also awarded the Luxembourg Croix de Guerre 1940–1945.

The M4A1(76)W Sherman Tank has a cast hull and turret. The tank was fitted with the late war Horizontal Volute Spring System (HVSS) suspension instead of the standard Vertical Volute Spring Suspension (VVSS). The new HVSS suspension was stronger than the VVSS. It was introduced to cope with the increase in tank weight because of the fitting of additional armour, larger gun and 23in wide, centre-guided tracks. New water-filled ammunition stowage boxes were fitted to each tank to reduce the chance of ammunition fires and explosions. The tank designation had the letter 'W' added to it to denote that wet stowage bins had been fitted. The M4A1 Sherman tank model was the first to be fitted with the high-velocity long-barrelled 76mm gun. It was fitted with a muzzle brake to help disperse the explosive gasses sideways when a shell was fired. It also increased the operational life of the gun barrel. Of the 3,426 produced, the British were sent 1,330 under the Lend-Lease scheme.

Specifications	
Dimensions:	L: 24ft 6in (7.46m); W: 8ft 9in (2.66m); H: 9ft 9in (2.97m); Wt: 31.5 tons (32 tonnes)
Engine:	Continental R975 C4 9-cylinder, 4-cycle, radial petrol/gasoline 460hp engine
Crew:	5
Main armament:	76mm M1A1, M1A1C or M1A2 in mount; M62 in turret
Additional weapons:	Two .30cal Browning MG M1919A4; .50cal Browning MG HB M2 AA mount; 2-inch Mortar M3 smoke bomb thrower
Armour thickness:	0.5in to 3.5in (12mm to 88.9mm)
Max. road speed:	21mph (33.79km/h)
Total built:	3,426

Chapter 41
M24 Chaffee Tank
Diekirch

Location: Set your navigation device to 10 Bamertal, 9209 Dikrech, Luxembourg. This is the Musée National d'Histoire Militaire Diekirch (National Museum of Military History). Be careful of the speed cameras.

The M24 Chaffee was intended to be the replacement for the failed M7 light/medium tank design. It replaced M3/M5 Stuart light tanks. It was a leap forward in light tank design and had modern torsion bar suspension, completely revised welded steel armour, improved protection and, more importantly, a much more powerful lightweight 75mm main gun. Although arriving late in the war, the Chaffee tank was a success. It was found to be efficient, simple, reliable and rugged. After the war, the tank was widely exported and stayed in service with many armies until the 1980s and beyond, encompassing most of the Cold War.

The M24 entered service with the US Army in the December of 1944. One of the first units to operate them was 740th Tank Battalion, which commandeered two recently arrived M24 Chaffee tanks. These two tanks first saw combat near Remouchamps on 20 December 1944. More vehicles entered service in 1945 as they became available. They continued to replace older Stuart light tanks until the end of the war.

At the end of World War Two, M24 Chaffee tanks, including this one, saw service with the Belgian Army. They were used as light reconnaissance Cavalry tanks. M24s started to be decommissioned in 1958 and were replaced by the M41 Walker Bulldog light tank. They were passed to reserve units. It was restored by the Bastogne Barracks Vehicle Restoration Centre in 2017 and lifted into its new location on 18 December 2018. It is displaying the marking of the US Army 19th Tank Battalion, 9th Armored Division.

The armour was not very thick. This kept the weight of the tank down. Tank crews had to rely upon speed to get them out of trouble. The front glacis plate was 1in (25mm) thick. The top of the hull was only 0.40 inch (10mm) thick. The sides of the hull sloped inwards at the bottom. The thickness of the armour on the hull side of the M24 Chaffee was not uniform: the front two thirds of the armour were 1in (25mm) thick, but the last third length of the side armour covering the engine compartment was only 0.75in (19mm) thick. The rear hull armour was 0.75in (19mm) thick. The turret armour was 1in (25mm) thick with the addition of a 1.5in (38mm) thick gun mantlet.

Specifications	
Dimensions:	L: 18ft 2in (5.54m); W: 9ft 8 in (2.98m); H: 9ft 1 in (2.77m); Wt: 20.2 tons (18.32 tonnes)
Engine:	Twin Cadillac 44T24 8-cylinder, 4-cycle, petrol/gasoline 148hp engine
Crew:	5
Main armament:	75mm M6 gun in mount; M64 in turret
Additional weapons:	Two .30cal Browning MG M1919A4; .50cal Browning MG M2HB
Armour thickness:	0.4in to 1.5in (10mm to 38mm)
Max. road speed:	35mph (56km/h)
Total built:	4,731

Chapter 42
M47 Patton Tank
Diekirch

Location: Set your navigation device to 10 Bamertal, 9209 Dikrech, Luxembourg. This is the Musée National d'Histoire Militaire Diekirch (National Museum of Military History). Be careful of the speed cameras.

Most of the exhibits and vehicles on display at the National Museum of Military History in Diekirch are from World War Two. The huge post-war, American-built M47 Patton tank that greets visitors by the museum's entrance seems to be out of place. What is not well known is that Luxembourg sent a contingent of troops to be part of the United Nations response to the invasion of South Korea by North Korean troops on 25 June 1950. Fifteen other UN member states would provide troops under a United Nations Joint Command. A total of 85 volunteer soldiers from Luxembourg joined the Belgian Battalion 'Belgian United Nations Command' (BUNC). Two Luxembourgish soldiers were killed in action in 1953 at Chokko-Ri. Near the end of the Korean war, some M47 Patton tanks were deployed to Korea for field testing. They did not see combat before the hostilities ended after the ceasefire armistice was signed on 27 July 1953. This tank is used as part of the annual Korean War commemoration ceremony to remember the Luxembourgish volunteers. It was cosmetically restored during the summer of 2018.

The M47 was designed in the late 1940s to replace the M4 Sherman, M26 Pershing and M46 Patton tanks. It was a stop-gap tank that only saw a few years of service in the US Army until it was replaced by the M48 Patton tank in 1953. The tank was rushed into production as the Korean War had started. To keep things simple, the M46 Patton tank's hull, engine, transmission, and drivetrain, were kept with minimal modifications. The tank hull was fitted with an M1919A4 Browning .30cal machinegun in a ball mount, and another was mounted in the turret next to the main gun. The M47 Patton was the last US medium tank to be armed with a bow machine gun.

The main change was the fitting of a new larger turret to house the 90mm gun. An M12 stereoscopic rangefinder was incorporated in the turret design. Production started in May 1952 at the Detroit Tank Arsenal and later at the American Locomotive Company. The M47 Patton tank was successfully exported to several countries around the world.

Specifications	
Dimensions:	L: 28ft 6in (8.68m); W: 11ft 11in (3.63m); H: 10ft 9in (3.27m); Wt: 53.5 tons (54.35 tonnes)
Engine:	Continental AVDS-1790-2A, 12-cylinder, supercharged diesel 750hp engine
Crew:	4
Main armament:	90mm gun in M87A1 mount
Additional weapons:	Two .30cal Browning M1919A4 machine guns; .50cal Browning M2 machine gun
Armour thickness:	2.36in to 7in (60mm to 178mm)
Max. road speed:	30mph (48.2km/h)
Total built:	8,576

Chapter 43

Jagdpanzer 38 (G13 Hetzer)
Diekirch

Location: Set your navigation device to 10 Bamertal, 9209 Dikrech, Luxembourg. This is the Musée National d'Histoire Militaire Diekirch (National Museum of Military History). Be careful of the speed cameras.

In 1982, the museum obtained a post-war, decommissioned, Swiss Army G13 Jagdpanzer 38 tank hunter. It was acquired to help tell the story of the Battle of the Bulge in Luxembourg. The G13 was altered to resemble a World War Two German Jagdpanther 38. Most of the Swiss Army additional features were removed, but not all. It can be easily identified as a G13 by spotting the two nuts, one on each curved section of the final drive to the left and right side of the front lower hull armour plate. The 75mm PaK 40 anti-tank gun with a muzzle brake was used to complete the Swiss contract order instead of the 75mm PaK 39 anti-tank gun mounted on the German Army Jagdpanzer 38 tank destroyers. The Škoda factory did not have access to the older PaK 39 guns and instead mounted the PaK 40. If you look at the end of the gun barrel, you will see the markings of where the gun brake used to be. It was removed and the vehicle painted in three-tone camouflage to make it look like a wartime German Jagdpanzer 38. Its Swiss serial number was M78027.

The Jagdpanzer 38 was not officially called the Hetzer by the Germans during World War Two. However, although most official wartime documents do not use the nickname 'Hetzer', a few did.

The Jagdpanzer 38s were assigned to Heeres Panzerjäger Abteilungen (Army Tank Hunter Battalions). They supported Infantry Divisions as a mobile anti-tank destroyer resource. When the infantry was under attack, they could be used as a resource to support the infantry's counter-attack. They were not intended to be used instead of a tank at the front of an attack in a major offensive and instead hunted in packs, never on their own and covered the flanks from concealed locations.

Overall, the vehicle was successful. It was quick and cheap to build compared with the cost of constructing a Tiger, King Tiger or Panther tank. It was mechanically reliable, easily hidden, hard-hitting, and when used right, a hard to kill vehicle. A company of Jagdpanzer 38 tank destroyers working together, concealed in a good location, could damage or knock-out a considerable number of attacking enemy tanks at long range.

Specifications	
Dimensions:	L: 20ft 7in (6.27m); W: 8ft 7in (2.63m); H: 6ft 11in (2.10m); Wt: 15.74 tons (16 tonnes)
Engine:	Praga EPA AC 2800 6-cylinder, petrol/gasoline 160hp engine
Crew:	4
Main armament:	7.5cm Pak 39 L/48
Additional weapons:	7.92mm M.G.34
Armour thickness:	0.3in to 2.4in (8mm to 60mm)
Max. road speed:	24.8mph (40km/h)
Total built:	2,612

Chapter 44

155mm Howitzer M2
Diekirch

Location: Set your navigation device to 10 Bamertal, 9209 Dikrech, Luxembourg. This is the Musée National d'Histoire Militaire Diekirch (National Museum of Military History). Be careful of the speed cameras.

Allied artillery was very effective in helping stop German Panzer divisions. During the Battle of the Bulge, the US Army field artillery was fully motorised. It had ample supplies of fuel and ammunition, unlike German Artillery batteries. The US Army had a much better fire control system and radios and field telephones were in a more plentiful supply. Troops on the frontline and artillery forward observation officers could send back grid references of concentrations of enemy troops and vehicles. Using a map, gun crews could calculate the settings and amount of propellant each shell needed to fire on the target. Typically, artillery crews could not see their target as it was too far away. They used indirect fire to lob shells over the heads of their own troops and tanks. The artillery relied on soldiers on the front line to tell them if the shells were on target or if the range needed to be adjusted. Artillery played a crucial role by bombarding Panzer divisions. When the weather improved, Allied air superiority enabled fire missions to be observed from above and corrections made by the crew of spotter aircraft. The heavy artillery bombardment on the Panzer divisions on the approaches to Elsenborn ridge caused many casualties, knocked out tanks and destroyed supply vehicles.

The 155mm Howitzer M2 was a towed artillery gun deployed by US Army field units in World War Two. It used two-part ammunition and could fire a 94.7lb (42.96 kg) high explosive M101 shell 14.6 miles (23.5km). The shell is rammed into the gun chamber to engage its rotating band into the barrel rifling. This was followed by the loading of the correct number of propellant powder bags that were needed to fire the shell at the desired distance. It could also fire smoke and armour-piercing ballistic cap high explosive APBC/HE shells. Under the Lend-Lease agreement, 182 were sent to Britain. It first saw combat in North Africa in December 1942 with A Battery 36th Field Artillery Battalion. The preferred prime mover was the tracked M4 High Speed Tractor. Early howitzers were mounted on the M1 carriage. This example is mounted on the later M2 carriage design.

Specifications	
Weight:	13.66 tons (13.88 tonnes)
Crew:	11–14
Main armament:	155mm Howitzer on M2 carriage
Maximum range:	14.6 miles (23.5km)
Shell:	94.7lb (42.96kg) high explosive M101 two-piece ammunition with bagged charge
Elevation:	-2 to +65 degrees
Traverse:	+60 degrees
Total built:	Over 1000

Chapter 45
M4 Sherman Tank
Wiltz

Location: Set your navigation device to 46 Route d'Ettelbruck, 9519 Wiltz, Luxembourg. You will see the tank on the other side of the road at the junction of Route de Bastogne and Route d'Ettelbruck.

This M4 Sherman tank is displayed as a memorial to the American soldiers that fought to liberate and then defend the attractive mediaeval town of Wiltz. In 2015, it was transported to the Bastogne Barracks Vehicle Restoration Center workshop to receive rust treatment and a new coat of paint. After the cosmetic restoration work was completed, the tank was returned to this new location in mid-July 2016.

This Sherman M4 tank has a cast nose and turret but welded hull. It is named after General Patton's nickname, 'Blood and Guts'. Notice that the driver's and machine hull gunner's head position has additional armour plating welded to the side. Two smaller additional plates of armour have been welded on the front hull armour in front of both men at head height for even more protection. On the right side, another piece of appliqué armour has been welded to the hull side to provide added protection to the ammunition stowage bins.

Its serial number 30270, RN 3038800 shows that it was manufactured by the Pullman Standard Company in May 1943. This tank belonged to the headquarters of Company B, 707th Tank Battalion and Lieutenant Colonel Ripple had used it as his command tank. On 16 and 17 December 1944, the 707th Tank Battalion fought in Marnach area, near Clervaux, where it suffered heavy losses. On 18 December, the surviving tanks were ordered to withdraw to Wiltz area. This tank was abandoned in Erpeldange (near Wiltz) on 19 December 1944. It was defending the Weidingen bridge prior to it being blown up by the US Army engineers. While manoeuvring from its position at the Café Halt, looking for a good firing position, it reversed into the Clees House and barn. The buildings collapsed onto the tank. It continued in reverse towards a house owned by the Keischler family, where it fell into a slurry pit in front of the farm and got stuck. The crew abandoned the tank but were captured by German soldiers, including Lieutenant Colonel Ripple. They were sent to a prisoner of war camp in Germany. In 1946, the tank was pulled out of the pit and moved to the Place des Martyrs in Wiltz town centre, where it remained as a war memorial for 70 years.

Specifications	
Dimensions:	L: 19ft 4in (5.89m); W: 8ft 7in (2.61m); H: 9ft (2.74m); Wt: 29.86 tons (30.34 tonnes)
Engine:	Continental R975 C1 9-cylinder, 4-cycle, radial petrol/gasoline 400hp engine
Crew:	5
Main armament:	75mm gun M3 in mount M34A1 in turret
Additional weapons:	Two .30cal Browning MG M1919A4; .50cal Browning MG HB M2 AA mount; 2-inch Mortar M3 smoke bomb thrower
Armour thickness:	0.5in to 3.5in (12mm to 88.9mm)
Max. road speed:	21mph (33.79km/h)
Total built:	6,748

Chapter 46

M4A3(76)W Sherman Tank
Clervaux

Location: Set your navigation device to Clervaux, Luxembourg. For many years, this tank stood on the forecourt of the Montée du Château castle in Clervaux. In 2019, it left this location to take part in some World War Two liberation anniversary events. In 2021, it was transported to the Bastogne Barrack's workshop to be cosmetically restored. The mayor of Clervaux announced that this vehicle would not return to the castle but that a new, yet to be disclosed, memorial site would be found for it in the centre of Clervaux. Contact the town's tourist office before planning your visit, to check that the Sherman has returned and where it is on display.

This surviving US Army M4A3(76) Sherman tank belonged to Company B, 2nd Tank Battalion, 9th Armored Division. It took part in the Battle of the Bulge.

Clervaux was the scene of heavy fighting. Units of the US Army's 110th Infantry Regiment, 28th Division dug in against advancing German Tanks and Panzer Grenadiers of the 2nd Panzer Division. On 17 December 1944, at about 11am, this Sherman tank was positioned in front of the Montée du Château castle gate in Clervaux. The crew had set up an ambush position behind an old stone-built mediaeval brewery. It moved a few metres forward, fired a shot from its 76mm main gun into the column of German tanks situated on the road near the cemetery and quickly backed up, taking cover behind the building. The crew repeated this manoeuvre again and again until it was damaged by return fire.

In 1956, the Luxembourg Army managed to tow the wreck into the castle courtyard through a hole in the damaged castle wall. There is battle damage on the gun mantlet and behind it on the right side of the turret. You can see a deep groove in the armour. Below that, there is the hole where a German shell penetrated the turret ring. This damage would have stopped the tank turret from turning and therefore forced the crew to abandon the vehicle. There could have been sharp metal splinters flying around inside the tank caused by the shell and resulting in destruction and injury.

Specifications	
Dimensions:	L: 24ft 9in (7.54m); W: 9ft 10in (2.99m); H: 9ft 9in (2.97m); Wt: 33.1 tons (33.65 tonnes)
Engine:	Ford GAA 8-cylinder, 4-cycle, petrol/gasoline 500hp engine
Crew:	5
Main armament:	76mm M1A1, M1A1C or M1A2 in mount M62 in turret
Additional weapons:	Two .30cal Browning MG M1919A4; .50cal Browning MG HB M2 AA mount; 2-inch Mortar M3 smoke bomb thrower
Armour thickness:	0.5in to 3.5in (12mm to 88.9mm)
Max. road speed:	26mph (41.8km/h)
Total built:	4,542

Bibliography

628th Tank Destroyer Battalion, After Action Report Dec. 1 to 31, 1944, United States Department of the Army

Doyle, Hilary Louis and Friedli, Lukas and Jentz, Thomas L, *Panzer Tracts No.4.3 Panzerkampfwagen IV Ausf.H and J 1943 to 45,* Panzer Tracts, Boyds, MD, USA (2016)

Doyle, Hilary Louis and Jentz, Thomas L, *Panzerkampfwagen IV Ausf.G, H and J 1942-45*, Osprey Publishing, Oxford (1955)

Guderian, Heinz Günther, *Das letzte Kriegsjahr im Westen – Die Geschichte der 116. Panzer Division Divisional War Diary of the II./146 - KTB II./Pz.Art.Rgt. 146*

Hunnicutt, R P, *Patton: A History of the American Main Battle Tank,* Echo Point Books and Media, Vermon (1978)

Hunnicutt, R P, *Sherman: A History of the American Medium Tank,* Echo Point Books and Media, Vermon (1978)

Hunnicutt, R P, *Stuart: A History of the American Light Tank,* Echo Point Books and Media, Vermon (1992)

MacDonald, Charles B, *The Definitive Account: The Battle of the Bulge,* Guild Publishing, London (1978)

Pallud, Jean Paul and Ramsey, Winston G, *Battle of the Bulge then and now,* Battle of Britain International Ltd, Essex (1984)

Wenkin, Hugues and Dujardin, Christian, *Les témoins d'acier tome I,* Belgium, Weyrich (2018)

Wenkin, Hugues and Dujardin, Christian, *Les témoins d'acier tome 2,* Belgium, Weyrich (2018)